Excel in Chinese

An Easy Starter 1

卓越汉语·轻松入门

主　　编：李如龙
副 主 编：杨子菁、吴　茗
参与编写人员：孟繁杰、王　颖、吴　琳、严　越
（按姓名音序排列）
英 文 翻 译：韩　臻、吴　琳

外语教学与研究出版社
FOREIGN LANGUAGE TEACHING AND RESEARCH PRESS
北京　BEIJING

图书在版编目(CIP)数据

卓越汉语. 轻松入门. 1/ 李如龙主编; 孟繁杰等编写. — 北京: 外语教学与研究出版社, 2011.11
外研社国际汉语培训教材. "卓越汉语"系列
ISBN 978-7-5135-1474-3

I. ①卓… II. ①李… ②孟… III. ①汉语—对外汉语教学—教材 IV. ①H195.4

中国版本图书馆 CIP 数据核字 (2011) 第 230127 号

出 版 人: 蔡剑峰
选题策划: 李彩霞
责任编辑: 李彩霞　刘虹艳
英文编辑: 蔡　莹
封面设计: 姚　军
版式设计: 北京锋尚制版有限公司
插图绘制: 华路天然图文设计工作室
出版发行: 外语教学与研究出版社
社　　址: 北京市西三环北路 19 号 (100089)
网　　址: http://www.fltrp.com
印　　刷: 北京方嘉彩色印刷有限责任公司
开　　本: 889×1194　1/16
印　　张: 11　插页: 0.25
版　　次: 2011 年 12 月第 1 版　2011 年 12 月第 1 次印刷
书　　号: ISBN 978-7-5135-1474-3
定　　价: 59.00 元(含 MP3 光盘一张)

*　*　*

购书咨询: (010)88819929　电子邮箱: club@fltrp.com
如有印刷、装订质量问题, 请与出版社联系
联系电话: (010)61207896　电子邮箱: zhijian@fltrp.com

物料号: 214740001

前 言

Preface

“卓越汉语”系列国际汉语培训教材是外研社针对非学历型外国学生在培训项目中学习基础汉语及专业汉语的实际需求，专门组织国内外多所高等院校及培训机构的教学专家编写，并全新推出的一整套教学资源解决方案。“卓越汉语·轻松入门”系列作为其中的综合性基础汉语培训教材，分为三册，是参照《国际汉语教学通用课程大纲》，结合国际汉语教学实际，以教学媒介语为英语的汉语学习者为对象编写的一套综合性快速入门教材。

一、编写思路

“卓越汉语·轻松入门”系列作为一套综合性的汉语教材，编写的主旨是帮助学习者掌握汉语语音、汉字、词汇、语法及中国文化方面的知识，培养学习者的汉语听说读写技能，使其具备用汉语进行基本言语交际的能力。在培养学习者言语交际技能的前提下，本系列教材重视汉语自身的特点，提倡以字带词、字词同步，常用先学，听说读写并进，尤其适合于希望快速、高效掌握汉语的学习者。

二、教材特色

1. 依据大纲，科学编写

“卓越汉语·轻松入门”系列由长期从事对外汉语教学的一线教师执笔，是一套依据《国际汉语教学通用课程大纲》编写的国际汉语教材。本教材趣味性强，版面活泼，注重汉外语言、文化对比，遵循第二语言教学规律，强调结构、功能、文化相结合，注重话题和知识点的循环推进，螺旋式地提高学生的汉语交际能力。

2. 常用先学，高频优先

本系列教材以中国的社会生活为背景，选取常用的交际功能项目以及学习者感兴趣的话题，按照常用先学的原则来确定功能项目出现的顺序，并尽量使各课的内容有一定的相关性。课文内容力求实用而有趣，选取在功能表达中最常用的词语、句型与语法点。

本系列教材依据“中国语言生活绿皮书”、《汉语水平词汇与汉字等级大纲》、《现代汉语频率词典》等多种频率数据，选取高频常用的字词作为教学内容，尤其是

“字、词、句”板块所选的汉字既高频又具有很强的构词能力，旨在提高词汇学习的效率，做到事半功倍。

3. 字词直通，以字带词

本系列教材根据汉语的特点，针对欧美学生读写方面的弱点，从第一册第6课开始设置“字、词、句”板块，选取本课出现的8—10个汉字，扩展为词、短语（包括自由短语）及短句。以字带词，既顾及汉字的书写训练，也强调字词关系。通过讲解汉字（汉语语素），帮助学生理解汉语词语的构成方式，提高词汇学习和运用的效率，培养汉语阅读能力。

4. 分册细致，课时灵活

考虑到国外汉语教学情况比较复杂，课时安排往往无法统一，每个学期的汉语课课时有限，学生程度又多参差不齐，本系列教材采用10课为一分册的方法来安排教学，一则可以使教材的适应面更广，二则方便在细分学生程度的基础上展开汉语教学。每10课为1册，每课6课时，每册60课时，复习考试6课时，完成每册约需66课时。本系列教材分3册，共约需200课时。学完之后学习者的汉语水平可达到《国际汉语教学通用课程大纲》二级。

使用说明

Introduction

《卓越汉语·轻松入门1》针对的是零起点的汉语学习者，共10课。根据教学侧重点不同，可以分为语音课(第1、第2课)、汉字课(第3—5课)和综合课(第6—10课)三大部分，教师可以根据学生的情况灵活选择。由于语音、汉字教学过程的特殊性，前5课的编写体例与其后各课有所不同，前5课都采用随堂操练的编写方式，每个知识点后附有随堂练习，最后配有供学生课后或学习新课前课堂复习使用的练习题。

第1、第2课以汉语拼音中声、韵、调的学习训练为主，训练形式多样，突破了传统教材语音训练较为枯燥的局限。同时，教学中引入少量常用短句，让学生在掌握语音知识的同时，能现学现用，开口说话。

第3—5课则以汉字的基础知识为主线，通过选取最能体现汉字造字规则的常用汉字，进行基础笔画、笔顺、部首及汉字结构的教学，同时进一步加深完善汉语拼音训练，进行语音部分连读音变（三声变调、轻声、儿化）的学习，并引入常用句型及课堂常用语，现学现用，提高学生的学习积极性。

第6—10课为综合课，每课主要设有下面5个板块。

1. 课文（含两段对话和一则短文）与生词板块

考虑到学习者来华学习、生活或工作的需要，本教材以中国为背景，以《国际汉语教学通用课程大纲》、“中国语言生活绿皮书”和《现代汉语频率词典》等为依据，选取常用的交际功能项目以及学习者感兴趣的话题进行编写，课文内容力求实用而生动有趣。课文中语言点也围绕功能的需要进行选取，尽量选取最常用的词语、句型和语法点，做到常用先学、急用先学。

主课文为两段对话和一篇短文，对话体和叙述体兼备，尽量做到内容实用、语言生动。主课文的学习可以结合后面的语言要点解析和练习进行，所需时间为2—3课时。

2. 语言要点解析板块

每课选取与功能点相关的语言要点进行讲解，从课文例句入手，通过汉英对比及句型类比分析，着重说明语义、结构和语用上应注意的问题，力求实用、明了。尽量不用或少用语言学术语，用简单形象的方法讲解语言知识，如通过例句、公式来介绍语言点。综合课每课讲解3—4个句型或语法点，第3册学完后，学习者将基本掌握汉语中的常用句型和语法项目。语言要点的讲练约为1—2课时。

3. 练习板块

主要分成五个部分，由易到难，循序渐进。

（1）语音练习。围绕课文内容，着重进行听力和发音训练，并给出一些相关的补充词汇。每课重点训练一个语音难点。

（2）语言点的练习。围绕重点词语、语法、句型展开训练，形式有选词填空、词语搭配、词语替换、重组句子、完成对话、用指定的句型改写句子、英译汉等。针对各语言点的特点和难点，设计不同形式的练习，以帮助学习者快速有效地了解语言点的语义和用法。

（3）课文内容练习。其主要形式有问答题、根据课文内容填空等，借助课文提供的语境，通过操练课文，帮助学生熟悉并且掌握语言点。

（4）功能点练习。着重选择与功能点相应的表达方式，设置情景让学生进行成段表述、看图完成会话等，并且将功能情景与本课所学语言点结合起来，使学生在掌握语言点之后，通过这些练习，进一步将语言能力转化为言语交际能力。

（5）课堂活动。本教材在丰富的个人练习基础上，增加群体性练习来展开和操练语言点，突出了第二语言课堂教学的特点。练习设计中将机械训练和互动训练相结合，语言结构训练和情景功能训练相结合，特别注重设计互动性练习来活跃课堂气氛，寓教于乐，教师可以根据实际教学的需要进行选用。

4. 字、词、句拓展板块

本教材针对欧美学生通常读写方面较弱的特点，综合课每课都设置“字、词、句”板块，采用就课选字、以字带词的形式，通过讲解汉字（汉语语素），帮助学生理解汉语词语的构成方式，从而提高词汇学习和运用的效率。主要内容分成三部分：

（1）汉字认读训练。选取每课课文中出现的8—10个必学汉字进行展示，将汉字扩展为词、短语（包括自由短语）及短句。强调汉语字词直通，培养学生的词语生成能力，帮助学生建立语素意识。所扩展的词、句一般都是常用词、句。如果出现生字，则标注拼音。要求学生记住汉字的意思，朗读扩展的词和句，如遇到没有学过的词，则根据汉字猜测它的意思，并查词典求证。

（2）汉字音义练习。通过强化汉字形、音、义之间的联系，促进学生对汉字的认知，同时拓展词汇学习的思路。练习形式有画线连接同一汉字的字形、字音、字义，还有组词、猜词义、认读生词卡片、辨字形标拼音等，以帮助学生进一步巩固字、词的学习。

（3）汉字书写练习。选取8—9个常用汉字，通过田字格展示每个字的笔画、笔顺和结构，帮助学生掌握正确的汉字书写方式。具体每个字的书写练习，可作为课后作业。

5. 文化知识板块

旨在结合课文内容介绍中国文化以及汉语基础知识，使学生在学习语言的同时，了解中国的语言文化、中国人的生活习俗等背景知识，引导学生从多元的角度来感受和理解中国文化，提高学生的学习兴趣。这一部分内容教师可在课堂上作简单介绍或扩展，也可作为学生课后的知识补充。教学上不作具体的要求。

汉语概说

A brief introduction to the Chinese language

汉语是世界上最古老的语言之一，也是当今世界上使用人数最多的语言，以汉语为母语的人口大约有14亿。汉语是联合国六种工作语言之一。在历史上，汉语还对日、韩等周边国家的语言文字产生过重要影响，如日语书面语中还保留着几千个源自中国的汉字。

Chinese is one of the oldest languages in the world. It has the biggest number of users in the world and is the native language of about 1.4 billion people. Chinese is also one of the 6 working languages of the UN. Throughout history Chinese had a great influence on the languages of surrounding countries such as Japan and the Republic of Korea. For example, written Japanese still has several thousand Chinese characters.

I "汉语"、"中文"和"普通话"的区别 The difference among "Hanyu", "Zhongwen" and "Putonghua"

中国不仅有汉族，还有55个少数民族。"汉语"，也叫"中文"，指的是汉族的语言文字，这两个词常常可以换用，但有时候"汉语"较侧重口语，"中文"更侧重书面语。中国疆域辽阔，在不同的地区，汉语有不同的分支，这些就是"方言"，比如"广东话"和"闽南语"等。汉语方言有七大方言区。不同方言之间除了有语音上的区别，词汇和语法也有一些不同，但书面语基本是统一的。在中国大陆地区，现代标准汉语称为"普通话"。有了"普通话"，来自不同方言区的人们才能方便地进行交流。本教材教的就是"普通话"。

Besides Han people, there are also 55 ethnic minorities living in China. "Hanyu", also known as "Zhongwen", refers to the language and characters of the Han ethnic group. These two words can usually replace each other. However, sometimes, "Hanyu" emphasizes spoken Chinese, while "Zhongwen" emphasizes written Chinese. China has a very vast territory. In different areas, "Hanyu" has different branches, which are "dialects", such as "Cantonese" and "Minnan dialect". There are 7 main dialect areas in China. Besides the difference in pronunciation, the dialects have different vocabulary and grammar too. But their written language is basically the same. In the mainland of China, the contemporary standard Chinese language is called "Putonghua". Speaking "Putonghua", people from different dialect areas can communicate with each other conveniently. This textbook teaches "Putonghua".

2 汉字和拼音 Chinese characters and Pinyin

1. 汉字 Chinese characters

汉字是汉语的书写符号，每个汉字都有自己的音、形、义。比如，汉字“明”，发音为“míng”，意义为“光明”。有时候，一个汉字有多个意义，如“明”还有“清楚”、“明白”的意思，一个汉字的多个意义之间常常有联系。大部分汉字是一字一音，但有时候，一个汉字有多个发音，如“还”有“hái”和“huán”两个发音，发“hái”音时，基本意义是“仍然”，发“huán”音时，基本意义是“归还”。

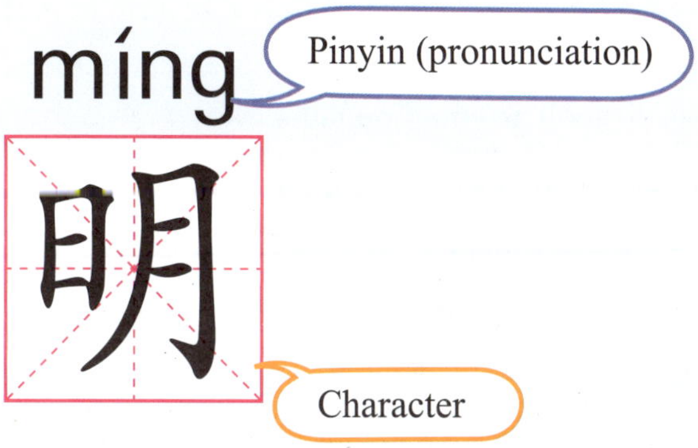

Chinese characters are the written form of Chinese language. Each character has its own pronunciation, form and meaning. For example, for the character “明”, its pronunciation is “míng” and its meaning is “bright”. Sometimes, one character has many meanings. For instance, character “明” also means “clear” or “understand”. The meanings of one character are usually related. Most characters have only one pronunciation. However, sometimes one character has more than one pronunciation. For example, character “还” has two pronunciations. When it’s pronounced as “hái”, the basic meaning is “still”; when it’s pronounced as “huán”, the basic meaning is “to return”.

汉字有几千年的历史，目前已发现的时代最早、体系较为完整的汉字是公元前14世纪殷商时代的甲骨文。最早的汉字是象形字，如“日(rì)”就是象太阳之形。但经过长时间的演变和改革，现代汉语中纯粹的象形字已经很少了，除了最早、最简单的独体字，如：日 (rì ⊙ sun)、人 (rén human)、山 (shān mountain)、水 (shuǐ water)等。

Chinese characters have a history of several thousand years. The earliest Chinese characters with a relatively complete system that are known today are oracle bone inscriptions of the Shang Dynasty in the 14th century B. C. The earliest characters are pictographs. For example, the character “日(rì)” resembles the sun. But after the evolution and reformation during thousands of years, there are not many wholly pictographic characters in the modern Chinese, except for the simplest and earliest characters, such as “日 (rì ⊙ sun)”, “人 (rén human)”, “山 (shān mountain)”, “水 (shuǐ water)”, etc.

现在，大多数汉字仍然有清晰的构字依据。比如，“明(míng)”，左边是“日(rì)”，意思为“太阳”，右边是“月(yuè)”，意思是“月亮”，合起来表示“光明”。多数汉字含一个声符和一个义符（即表义的部首），如“爸(bà)”上边的“父(fù)”是义符，表示“父亲”，下边的“巴(bā)”是声符，提示了这个字的发音。只要学好了汉字部件和结构，你就会发现，书写汉字并不是一件很难的事儿。

Now, most of the Chinese characters still have clear construction rules. For example, character "明(míng)" has "日(rì)" on the left side which means the sun, and "月(yuè)" on the right side which means the moon. Putting the sun and the moon together expresses the meaning of "bright". Most characters are composite of phonetic components and semantic radicals. Character "爸(bà)" has "父(fù)" on the top which means father and "巴(bā)"at the bottom which indicates the pronunciation. As long as you master the radicals and structures, you will discover that writing Chinese characters is not as difficult as you thought.

2. 拼音 Pinyin

拼音是用罗马字母来拼写汉语语音的系统，发布于20世纪50年代。汉语音节的基本结构如右图：

Pinyin is the Romanized phonetic spelling system for standard Chinese, which was created in the 1950s. The basic structure of a Chinese syllable is shown in the picture on the right:

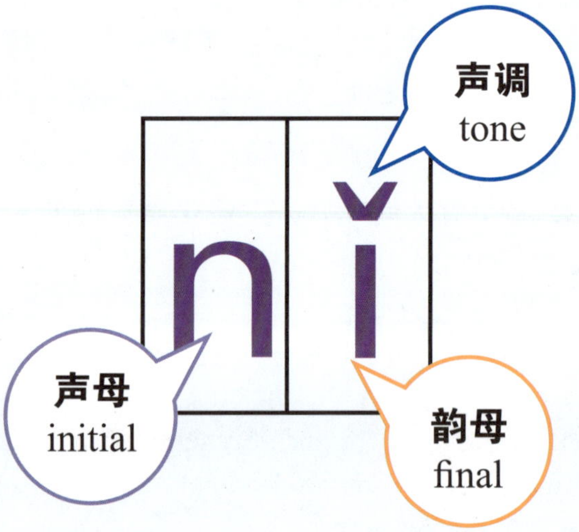

每个汉字对应一个汉语音节，音节由声母（shēngmǔ）、韵母（yùnmǔ）和声调（shēngdiào）构成。汉语拼音一共有21个声母，36个韵母（包含卷舌元音韵母er），4个声调（不包含"轻声"）。

Each Chinese character corresponds to one syllable. A syllable consists of an initial, a final and a tone. There are totally 21 initials, 36 finals (including the retroflex final er) and 4 tones (not including the "neutral tone") in Chinese Pinyin system.

3. 为什么不用拼音取代汉字作为汉语的书写系统？ Why not replace Chinese characters with Pinyin as the Chinese writing system?

用拼音取代汉字作为汉语的书写系统是不可能的，因为汉语中有太多的同音字。比如，有三十多个汉字的发音都为"shì"，但每个汉字都有其不同的意思。再如，"明(míng)"的意思是"光明"，"名(míng)"的意思是"名字"，"鸣(míng)"的意思是"叫"，"茗(míng)"的意思则是"茶"。

It is impossible to replace Chinese characters with Pinyin as the Chinese writing system, because there are too many homophonic characters in Chinese. For example, there are more than 30 characters that are pronounced as "shì", but every character has its own meaning. Another example, "明(míng)" means "bright", "名(míng)" means "name", "鸣(míng)" means "chirp", while "茗(míng)" means "tea".

4. 要学习多少汉字？ How many Chinese characters do you need to study?

大型汉语字典的收字量大约在5万到8万，但是，常用汉字只有3500个。统计资料显示，只要掌握934个汉字就能看懂汉语语料的90%。一般说来，只要学会300个汉字就能掌握基本的生活用语。

There are about 50,000~80,000 entries for Chinese characters in Chinese dictionaries. But only 3,500 of them are frequently used. According to the statistics, if you know 934 characters, you can read 90% of Chinese reading materials. Generally speaking, 300 of the most commonly used characters can help you survive in Chinese daily life.

3 汉字和词的关系 Relationship between Chinese characters and words

古代汉语以单音节词为主，现代汉语以双音节词为主。据统计，《现代汉语词典》中双音节词占词语总数的62%。

Ancient Chinese words are mainly single-syllable (one character), while modern Chinese words are mainly double-syllable (two characters). According to the statistics, 62% of words in *The Contemporary Chinese Dictionary* are double-syllable words.

汉字和词的关系非常密切，一个词的意义往往与合成该词的汉字的意义分不开，例如，"学费(xuéfèi tuition)" = "学(xué study; learn)" + "费(fèi cost; fee)"。学会了一个汉字，往往可以推知很多词和短语的意思，做到事半功倍。

Chinese characters and words are very closely related. Usually, the meaning of a word is highly related to the meanings of its characters. For example, "学费(xuéfèi tuition)" = "学(xué study; learn)" + "费(fèi cost; fee)". After learning one character, you can know the meanings of many words and phrases by inference. Get twice the result with half the effort.

例如 (For example):

学(xué study) + 生(shēng student) = 学生(student)

学(xué study) + 期(qī period of time) = 学期(semester)

学(xué study) + 汉语(Hànyǔ Chinese) = 学汉语(study Chinese)

4 语法 Grammar

汉语没有表示语法意义的词形变化，如：

Chinese has no inflection that indicates grammar differences. For example:

English	Chinese
study; studied; studying	学(xué)
semester; semesters	学期(xuéqī)
I; me	我(wǒ)

但在汉语中，语序非常重要，词的顺序不同，句子的意义也相应地发生变化，如：

But the order of words is very important in Chinese. Different orders of words make different meanings of the sentences. For example:

Chinese sentences	English meanings
Ài wǒ de rén wǒ bú ài 爱我的人我不爱。	I don't love the person who loves me.
Wǒ ài de rén bú ài wǒ 我爱的人不爱我。	The person whom I love doesn't love me.

汉语中虚词非常重要，如"着(zhe)"、"了(le)"。

Function words are very important in Chinese, for example,"着(zhe)" and "了(le)".

Chinese sentences	English meanings
Tā kàn zhe zhè běn shū 他看着这本书。	He is reading this book.
Tā kàn le zhè běn shū 他看了这本书。	He has read this book.

汉语中还有很多量词。数词和名词中间，一般必须有量词，如：

There are many measure words in Chinese. They are usually used between numerals and nouns. For example:

Numerals	Measure words	Nouns
yī 一 one	ge 个	rén 人 person
liǎng 两 two	ge 个	xuésheng 学生 students
sān 三 three	běn 本	shū 书 books

目 录 | CONTENTS

	题目	功能任务	学习要点	文化知识	页码
第一课 Lesson 1	语音（一） Phonetics (1)	简单问候（你好）	1. 韵母：ɑ o e i u ü ɑi ei ɑo ou ɑn en ɑng eng ong 2. 声母：b p m f d t n l g k h 3. 声调：汉语的声调和标调规则 (1)	汉语基本知识	1
第二课 Lesson 2	语音（二） Phonetics (2)	简单道谢（谢谢）、道歉（对不起）、告别（再见）	1. 韵母：以 i、u、ü开头的复韵母和鼻韵母及卷舌元音韵母er 2. 声母：j q x z c s zh ch sh r 3. 声调：标调规则 (2)	数字	17
第三课 Lesson 3	汉字（一） Characters (1)	日常（课堂）用语（一）	1. 汉字：人、日、月、目、口、山、水、大、天、火 的意义及写法 2. 汉字基本笔画 3. 汉字基本笔顺 4. 语音：三声变调	汉字带来的灵感	33
第四课 Lesson 4	汉字（二） Characters (2)	日常（课堂）用语（二）	1. 汉字：木、林、本、上、下、明、相、泪、文、白、百、小、少 的意义及写法 2. 语音：轻声	汉字的构成（一）	47
第五课 Lesson 5	汉字（三） Characters (3)	日常（课堂）用语（三）	1. 汉字：米、来、刀、力、田、手、心、女、子、门、好、男、问、想的意义及写法 2. 汉字基本结构 3. 语音：儿化	汉字的构成（二）	57

	题目	功能任务	语言要点	文化知识	页码
第六课 Lesson 6	你好！ Hello!	初次见面（介绍姓名、询问姓名）；熟人寒暄	1. S + adv. + adj.：我很忙。 2. “……吗？”：你忙吗？ 3. “……呢？”：我叫马丁。你呢？	中国人的姓名	69
第七课 Lesson 7	我介绍一下 Allow me to introduce you to each other	自我介绍、介绍朋友、询问国籍	1. ……是……：我是美国人。 2. pron./n. + 的 + n.：我的朋友 3. “也”的用法：他也学习汉语。	中国人的称谓	81
第八课 Lesson 8	她是谁？ Who is she?	看照片介绍家庭成员	1. 用“谁”提问：她是谁？ 2. ……有/没有……：我有哥哥，没有姐姐。 3. A和B：我爸爸、妈妈、弟弟和妹妹在美国。	中国人的亲属称谓	93
第九课 Lesson 9	你做什么工作？ What do you do?	询问和介绍职业、专业	1. 用“什么”提问：你做什么工作？ 2. “都”的用法：我们都是中文系的学生。 3. 量词（一）：个、位	打招呼	105
第十课 Lesson10	苹果多少钱一斤？ How much are the apples?	问答商品价格、讨价还价、付款	1. 1—100的基本数词 2. 人民币的写法和读法 3. “太 + adj. + 了”：太贵了！ 4. “几”和“多少”	中国的货币	117

课文英文翻译 English translation of the texts 131

练习答案 Answers to exercises 134

总字表 Character list 153

生词表 Vocabulary list 156

第一课 Lesson 1
语音（一）Phonetics (I)

学习要点

1 韵母：a o e i u ü
ai ei ao ou
an en ang eng ong

2 声母：b p m f d t n l g k h

3 声调：汉语的声调和标调规则（1）

一 韵母 | Finals

a o e i u ü	ai ei ao ou	an en ang eng ong

1 单韵母 The “singles” (simple finals)

a o e i u ü

发音与英语大致对应的单韵母有：

The simple finals that approximately correspond to their English “counterparts” are:

拼音	a	e	i	u
英语	father	girl	he	who

提示 Be aware

① e

汉语的e比英语的“her”口形略扁，接近“girl、bird”。

The mouth shape of the Chinese Pinyin “e” is like its “counterpart” in the English words “girl, bird”, and is a bit flatter than its “counterpart” in the word “her”.

② i

汉语的i的发音不完全等同于英语单词“he”中的“e”的发音。汉语的i上下齿靠近，嘴角外拉，呈紧张状态。英语“he”中的“e”发音时嘴角不外拉。

The pronunciation of “i” is not exactly the same as that of “e” in the English word “he”. The mouth shape of “i” is still flatter, with the corners of the mouth stretched aside and strained a little; while to utter the “e” in “he”, one does not stretch aside both lips.

③ u

汉语的u唇形圆而突出。

When pronouncing “u”, lips are rounded and protruded.

④ o

o比u口形大一点点。

When pronouncing “o”, lips are slightly looser than pronouncing “u”.

⑤ ü

可先发i音，再把嘴唇逐渐拢圆，之后的延长音就是ü。或者先发u音，再把舌面向前伸也一样得到ü。i和ü的发音方法如下图所示：

Let’s start with “i”. Then round your lips up gradually and the prolonged part is just “ü”. Or you can start with “u”. Reach your tongue forward without changing the lip shape and there would come “ü”. The mouth shape of “i” and “ü” is shown below:

⑥ 请注意，这6个基本元音的开口度一个比一个小。

Please note that the opening of the six basic vowels becomes smaller all the way down from “ɑ” to “ü”.

ɑ o e i u ü

2 复韵母 The “couples” (compound finals)

ɑi ei ɑo ou

在ɑi、ei、ɑo、ou之中，前后两个音的轻重是不同的。处于前面的ɑ、e、ɑ、o（主要元音）是强音，发音较长；而处于后面的i、o、u是弱音，发音较短。

In “ɑi, ei, ɑo, ou”, the first vowels are pronounced stronger and longer than the second ones.

提示 Be aware

① **拼合技巧** Notes on combination

跟英语相比，汉语中的复韵母听起来更像一个板块，基本分辨不出内部由一个元音滑向另一个元音的过程。如果把汉语的复韵母发成像英语那样，会显得比较夸张。

Compared with their English “counterparts”, the Chinese compound finals sound more like whole chunks, making it hard to tell the sliding from one vowel to another. If the Chinese compound finals were pronounced in the English way, it would sound exaggerated.

以下发音只是模糊对应，差别不难听出。

The following pairs of pronunciations are only vaguely corresponding to each other. And the difference is obvious.

拼音	ɑi	ei	ɑo	ou
英语	b<u>y</u>	th<u>ey</u>	h<u>ow</u>	g<u>o</u>

② ai、ei

韵母ai中a的开口度比英语单词“bed”中的“e”大，而又比英语“bad”中的“a”小。韵母ei的发音有点像英语字母“a”的发音。

The “a” in final “ai” is more open than the “e” in the English word “bed”, but smaller than the “a” in “bad”. “ei” is somehow like the pronunciation of the English letter “a”.

随堂练 Classroom exercises

1. 读一读这些韵母。Read these finals.

a	o	e	i	u	ü
ai	ei	ao	ou		

ei	e	ao	ai
i	ü	o	ou
a	ao	u	ü

2. 听老师的发音，写下韵母，并跟读。Listen to the teacher, write down the finals, and read after the teacher.

____ ____ ____ ____ ____ ____ ____ ____ ____ ____

3. 辨别对错。指出老师的发音是对的还是错的，如果是错的，请说出正确的发音。
True/False. Tell true or false about the teacher’s pronunciation and correct the wrong ones.

o　　i　　a　　e　　u　　ü

ou　　ei　　ao　　ai

课堂活动 Activities

1. 语音抢答：听老师的发音，抢答老师所说的是6个单韵母中的哪一个。
Listen to the teacher and point out the one pronounced by the teacher from the 6 simple finals — the faster, the better.

2. 一个说，一个写：先请A同学到黑板前，背对全班同学，然后老师举某一张拼音卡，指定B同学发音，让A同学写出相对应的拼音。

One reads and one writes: First ask student A to the blackboard with his back to the class. Then the teacher raises Pinyin cards one by one, and asks student B to dictate student A.

3 鼻韵母 The nasals

an en ang eng ong

“n”韵尾很像英语单词“an、ten”中“n”的发音。an、en发音时，先发元音，紧接着舌尖往上齿龈移动，最后抵住上齿龈。ang、eng、ong发音时，先发元音，紧接着舌根往软腭移动并抵住软腭发ng。ang中的a比单韵母a开口大些。

The “n” end is like the “n” sound in the English words “an, ten”. To pronounce “an, en”, make the vowel first, and then move the tip of your tongue upward and touch the gum of your upper teeth. To pronounce “ang, eng, ong”, make the vowel first, and then move the root of your tongue toward the soft palate and touch against it. The “a” in “ang” is with more opening than the simple final “a”.

提示 Be aware

注意分辨 Differentiation

前鼻音	an	en	nnnnnnn…
后鼻音	ang	eng	ŋŋŋŋŋŋŋ…

随堂练 Classroom exercises

1. 听老师的发音，写下韵母，并跟读。Listen to the teacher, write down the finals, and read after the teacher.

_____ _____ _____ _____ _____

2. 辨别对错。指出老师的发音是对的还是错的，如果是错的，请说出正确的发音。

True/False. Tell true or false about the teacher's pronunciation and correct the wrong ones.

ong　　en　　ang　　eng　　an

课堂活动
Activities

1. 左手还是右手：听老师的发音，如果是A音请举左手，如果是B音请举右手。做完后再读一读A、B两组，注意二者的区别。

   Left hand or right hand: Listen to the teacher and raise your hand accordingly — left hand for Column A and right hand for Column B. Then read the two columns and pay attention to their differences.

A	an	an	en	ang	eng
B	ang	en	eng	eng	ong

2. 一个说，一个写：先请A同学到黑板前，背对全班同学，然后老师举某一张拼音卡，指定B同学发音，让A同学写出相对应的拼音。

   One reads and one writes: First ask student A to the blackboard with his back to the class. Then the teacher raises Pinyin cards one by one, and asks student B to dictate student A.

二 声母 | Initials

b　p
m　f

d　t
n　l

g　k　h

1 发音与英语一致的声母 The initials sharing the same pronunciation with their English "counterparts"

拼音	m	f	n	l
英语	me	fee	need	let

随堂练 Classroom exercises

听录音，看图片，填出声母。Listen to the recording, look at the pictures, and fill in the initials.

____āo
cat

____ā
mother

____ō
touch

____ǎi
____ai
grandma

____ēi
fly

____ā
drag

2 发音与英语能基本对应（≠完全对应）的声母 The initials approximately corresponding to their English "counterparts"

拼音	b	p	d	t	g	k	h
英语	speak/web	pie	stop/bed	to	sky/dog	key	hi

提示　Be aware

① 与英语相应发音相比，b、d、g和p、t、k都是清音，声带不振动。

Compared to their English "counterparts", "b, d, g" and "p, t, k" in Chinese are all unvoiced sounds, meaning there is no vibration of the vocal cord.

② b、d、g不送气（呼出气流较弱），p、t、k送气（呼出气流较强）。

"b, d, g" are unaspirated consonants, which are pronounced with very weak breath; while "p, t, k" are aspirated ones with stronger breath.

不送气	b	d	g	unaspirated
送气	p	t	k	aspirated

③ h

与英语的"h"相比，h发音时舌根要抬高，声带不振动。

Compared to the English letter "h", the "h" in Chinese is produced with the root of the tongue raised and there is no vocal cord viberation.

随堂练 Classroom exercises

1. 听老师的发音，写下声母，并跟读。Listen to the teacher, write down the initials, and read after the teacher.

___o, ___o　　___o, ___o　　___e, ___e　　___e, ___e

___e, ___e　　___i, ___i　　___a, ___a　　___u, ___u

___ai, ___ai　　___ei, ___ei　　___ao, ___ao　　___ou, ___ou

___an, ___ang　　___en, ___eng　　___eng, ___ong

2. 辨别对错。指出老师的发音是对的还是错的，如果是错的，请说出正确的发音。

True/False. Tell true or false about the teacher's pronunciation and correct the wrong ones.

bu　　dai　　da　　gai

tou　　ke　　ta　　ku

课堂活动 Activities

1. 左手还是右手：听老师的发音，如果是A音请举左手，如果是B音请举右手。做完后再读一读A、B两组，注意二者的区别。

   Left hand or right hand: Listen to the teacher and raise your hand accordingly — left hand for Column A and right hand for Column B. Then read the two columns and pay attention to their differences.

A	ban	dai	gen	gou	nei	ma	fo	mo	he
B	pan	tai	ken	kou	lei	fa	fou	mou	hei

2. 听音举牌：听老师的发音，然后举起手中相对应的拼音卡片。

   Raise the Pinyin cards at hand according to the teacher's pronunciation.

3. 看卡片抢答：分成两个小组，看老师手中举的拼音卡片，迅速发音，最先答对者计1分。

   Divide the class into two groups. The teacher raises Pinyin cards one by one and asks students to pronounce them as quickly as possible. The fastest one who gives the correct answer scores one point.

三 声调 | Tones

ask－wèn
kiss－wěn

<u>Wǒ</u> <u>xiǎng</u> <u>wen</u> <u>nǐ</u>.

I wanna ask you?
I wanna kiss you?

1 汉语的声调 The tones in Chinese

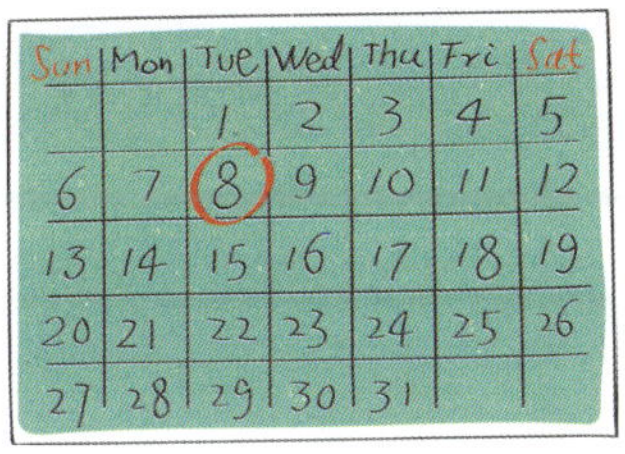

bā（eight）

bá（pull out）

bǎ（target）

bà（father）

汉语的声调主要由音高的变化构成。声调具有区别意义的作用，因此掌握声调非常重要。汉语共有四个声调：一声（—）、二声（/）、三声（V）、四声（\），音高升降变化如下图所示：

The tones in Chinese refer to the pitch variation within a syllable. Different tones indicate different meanings, so it is necessary to master the rules of tones.There are 4 tones in Chinese: the 1st tone (—), the 2nd tone (/), the 3rd tone (V) and the 4th tone (\). The pitch of each tone is shown below:

四声图 4 Tones

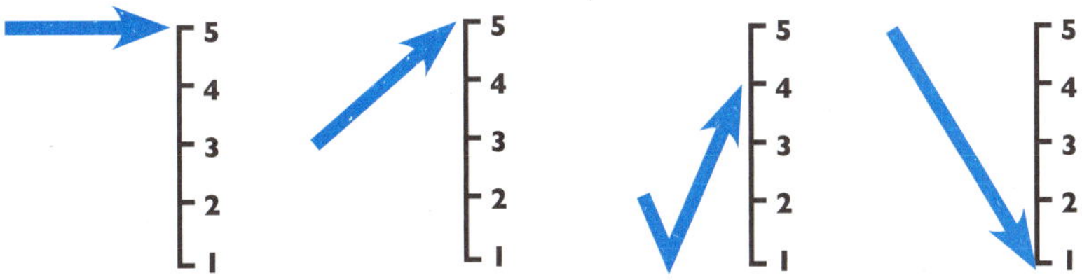

（55）　（35）　（214）　（51）

▶ 提示 Be aware

对于声调来说，绝对音高并不重要（因为每个人的音域不同），重要的是相对音高。所以如果你发的一声比别人的高或低，不要紧张，只要你的一声发得又高又平，而且能够与其他三声区别开来，就足够了。

The pitch of the tones is not an absolute standard as it varies with individuals' voice. The point is the relative pitch of tones. Take it easy if you happen to find that your first tone sounds higher or lower than that of others. As long as the first tone is uttered high and flat, and could be differentiated from the other three tones, it's all right.

随堂练
Classroom exercises

1. 朗读并辨义(注意：声调不同，表达的意义不同)。Read and tell the meanings. (Pay attention to the variation of meanings brought by different tones.)

mā
mother

má
hemp

mǎ
horse

mà
curse

tāng
soup

táng
sugar

tǎng
lie

tàng
boiling hot

2. 练习发音。Practice the pronunciations.

b	（ā	á	ǎ	à）	→	bā	bá	bǎ	bà
m	（ō	ó	ǒ	ò）	→	mō	mó	mǒ	mò
k	（ē	é	ě	è）	→	kē	ké	kě	kè
d	（ī	í	ǐ	ì）	→	dī	dí	dǐ	dì
g	（ē	é	ě	è）	→	gē	gé	gě	gè
l	（ū	ú	ǔ	ù）	→	lū	lú	lǔ	lù
n	（ā	á	ǎ	à）	→	nā	ná	nǎ	nà

2 标调规则（1）Rules for marking tones (I)

声调符号要标在音节中的元音上。当一个音节只有一个元音时，声调符号就标在这个元音上，如bǎ、mō。当一个音节有两个或两个以上的元音时，声调符号标在开口度大的那个元音上，如tào、bēi。

The tone mark always falls on a vowel of the syllable. When there is only one vowel in a syllable, the tone is marked on top of the only vowel, for example “bǎ, mō”. When there are two or more vowels, the tone mark falls on top of the vowel with bigger opening, such as “tào, bēi”.

提示　Be aware

i 上有调号时要去掉i上的点儿，如bǐ、ní。

When the tone mark falls on top of “i”, the dot of “i” is removed (to give place to the tone mark), such as in “bǐ”and “ní”.

随堂练 Classroom exercises

1. 声韵调拼合练习。请拼合以下声母、韵母和声调。Practice combination. Please combine the following initials, finals and tones.

d	ōu;	m	áng;	g	è;	w	ǒ;	n	ǚ;
l	ù;	m	ǎi;	d	ōng;	l	èi;	t	éng

2. 听老师朗读拼音，标出声调。Listen to the teacher and mark the tones.

da　lü　gai　mei　lao　hou　hen　hong

dahong　dalou　hongdeng　heiban　hengao

课堂活动 Activities

1. 听音演示调号：由老师或某个同学发音，其他学生用肢体语言来演示四声。

Listen and pose: Show the four tones with your body language according to the sounds pronounced by the teacher or a student.

2. 听写比赛。

Dictation competition.

四 练习 | Exercises

1. 唱四声。Read the four tones aloud.

bāi	bái	bǎi	bài
pāi	pái	pǎi	pài
fēi	féi	fěi	fèi
mō	mó	mǒ	mò
pāo	páo	pǎo	pào
māo	máo	mǎo	mào
hān	hán	hǎn	hàn
fān	fán	fǎn	fàn

dī	dí	dǐ	dì
tū	tú	tǔ	tù
nān	nán	nǎn	nàn
lēi	léi	lěi	lèi
gēn	gén	gěn	gèn
kē	ké	kě	kè
fēn	fén	fěn	fèn
hōu	hóu	hǒu	hòu

2. 读音节。Read the syllables aloud.

bā pà dǎ dà tā tǎ nǐ lǐ

mò fó dōu tōu gǒu kǒu hǒu dōng dǒng

3. 读短句。Read the short sentences aloud.

Nǐ lèi ma?	Are you tired?
Hěn lèi.	Very tired.
Nǐ è ma?	Are you hungry?
Hěn è.	Very hungry.
Nǐ kě ma?	Are you thirsty?
Hěn kě.	Very thirsty.
Nǐ lái ma?	Will you come?
Wǒ bù lái.	I won't come.
Tā hěn ài nǐ.	He loves you very much.

4. 听老师的发音，写下声母，并注意每组发音的区别。Listen to the teacher, write down the initials and differentiate the similar pronunciations in each pair.

__ǎo	__ǎo	__í	__í	__ú	__ú	__ēng	__ēng
__ài	__ài	__uó	__uó	__ǐng	__ǐng	__ōu	__ōu
__ōng	__ōng	__è	__è	__ǔ	__ǔ	__àn	__àn
__ǎn	__ǎng	__ān	__āng	__én	__éng	__ēn	__ēng

5. 听录音填写声母。Listen to the recording and fill in the initials.

__āng__áng	__ě__éng	__í__ū	__í__āi
__ǔ__ài	__ā__á	__ài__ù	__ēi__ǎn

6. 听录音填写韵母和声调。Listen to the recording and fill in the finals and tones.

n____r____	sh____h____	z____l____	l____l____
d____f____	h____h____	m____m____	h____ch____

五 现学现用 | Survival Chinese

在中国，跟认识的人或不认识的人打招呼，都可以说"你好(nǐ hǎo)"。但"你好"稍显正式，所以跟家人或关系亲密的朋友打招呼时较少用到。

In China, "你好(nǐ hǎo)" can be used for greeting both acquaintances and strangers. But it somehow sounds formal, so it is not frequently used when one greets his/her families or close friends.

课堂活动
Activities

传花说“你好”：老师将手中的花（或其他小物件）扔给第一个学生，说：“你好，××（名字）。”该学生将花递给自己身边的同学，并传递问候。

Pass the flowers and say hello. The teacher throws flowers (or other things) to the first student and says, “Nǐ hǎo, ×× (the name).” The student who gets the flowers passes them to the next one, saying hello at the same time.

文化知识
Chinese ABC

汉语基本知识
Basic Knowledge of Chinese

The Chinese characters serve as the written system of the Chinese language; while the role of Pinyin is only the phonetic symbol of the Chinese language, just as the International Phonetic Alphabets are applied to indicate the pronunciation of English words in the dictionary for learners. One character normally corresponds to one syllable. A Chinese syllable is theoretically composed of three parts: the initial, the final and the tone. For instance, in “bā”, “b” is the initial, “a” is the final, and “–” indicates the tone. Tones differentiate meanings. For example, “mā” (mum), “má” (hemp), “mǎ” (horse) and “mà” (to curse).

In Mandarin, the standard modern Chinese language, there are over four hundred syllables. The number is only over one thousand and two hundred, when all those syllables are combined with different tones. As a result, it becomes a universal phenomenon in Chinese that one pronunciation indicates various meanings. Context helps with ambiguity clarification in oral communication; while in the written one, it is Chinese characters that differentiate meanings. That is, the various meanings of the same syllable could be indicated by different character forms. It can be said that the reason why Chinese characters, having experienced several thousand years of ups and downs, still show exuberant vitality. During thousands of years of history, the Chinese phonetic system has gone through great changes, but the Chinese characters have not changed much. The dialect areas have differences in their phonetic systems, yet they use the same Chinese characters. In this way, Chinese characters can be used as communication tools in different historical periods as well as dialect areas.

第二课 Lesson 2

语音（二）Phonetics (2)

学习要点

1 韵母：以 i、u、ü开头的复韵母和鼻韵母及卷舌元音韵母er

2 声母：j q x z c s zh ch sh r

3 声调：标调规则（2）

一 韵母 | Finals

ia ie iao iou(iu)
ua uo uai uei(ui)
üe

ian in iang ing iong
uan uen(un) uang ueng
üan ün

er

1 以i、u、ü 开头的复韵母和鼻韵母 The "i–", "u–", "ü–" columns

	a	o	e
i	ia		ie
u	ua	uo	
ü			üe

	ai	ei	ao	ou
i			iao	iou(iu)
u	uai	uei(ui)		
ü				

	an	en	ang	eng	ong
i	ian	in	iang	ing	iong
u	uan	uen(un)	uang	ueng	
ü	üan	ün			

[表格说明] 1. 带（ ）的是与声母拼合时的省略写法。
2. 表中空位说明实际发音中不存在该拼合。

[Caption] 1. The finals in the brackets are the abbreviated spelling form.
2. The blank space in the table indicates that there is no such pronunciation in Chinese.

提示 Be aware

① **拼合技巧** Notes on combination

以i、u、ü开头的复韵母和鼻韵母，开头的i、u、ü是弱音，发音较短；后面的元音才是主要元音，读强音，发音较长。以下发音只是模糊对应：

In a compound final or nasal started with “i, u, ü” like “i, u, ü + vowel (+ n/ng)”, the “i, u, ü” at the beginning is weak and short; while the following vowel is the main vowel, which is stronger and longer. Below is only some approximate correspondence:

拼音	ia	ie	in	ing	uai	uei	uan
英语	yard	yes	sin	sing	why	way	one

② ian和üan中的a比单韵母a的口形略扁。同样，ie和üe中的e也比单韵母e略扁。

In “ian” and “üan”, the “a” is produced with a comparatively flatter shape of the mouth than “a” as a simple vowel. Similarly, in “ie” and “üe”, the “e” is produced with a comparatively flatter mouth shape than “e” as a simple vowel.

③ “i-” 列与 “ü-” 列发音不同。“i-” 列为不圆唇音，“ü-” 列为圆唇音。

The pronunciations of “i-” column and “ü-” column are different. “i-” column is pronounced with unrounded lips, while “ü-” column is pronounced with rounded lips.

不圆唇	i	ie	in	ian
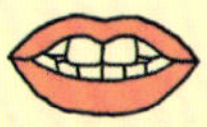				
圆唇	ü	üe	ün	üan
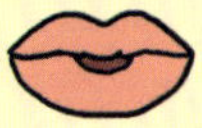				

④ 汉语的韵母有时可以自成音节，如：é（鹅 goose）、ài（爱 to love）。但是i、u、ü独立成音节时，应记为yi、wu、yu。以i、u、ü开头的韵母独立成音节时，拼写规则如下：

Some Chinese syllables consist of only a final and a tone, like é (鹅 goose) and ài (爱 to love). But when "i, u, ü" serve as independent syllables without an initial before, the spellings are "yi, wu, yu". The spelling rules for finals started with "i, u, ü" as independent syllables are here:

i	i in ing	yi yin ying	Add "y"
	ia ie iao iou ian iang iong	ya ye yao you yan yang yong	Change "i" to "y"
u	u	wu	Add "w"
	ua uo uai uei uan uang uen ueng	wa wo wai wei wan wang wen weng	Change "u" to "w"
ü	ü üe üan ün	yu yue yuan yun	Add "y", and remove the two dots on the "ü"

⑤ **注意分辨** Differentiation

前鼻音	ian	uan	in	uen(un)
后鼻音	iang	uang	ing	ueng

nnnnnnn…

ŋŋŋŋŋŋŋ…

⑥ iou、uei、uen 前有声母时，写为 iu、ui、un。如：

With an initial before, "iou, uei, uen" are spelt as "iu, ui, un". For example:

j + iou → jiu　　d + uei → dui　　h + uen → hun

2 卷舌元音韵母 The retroflex final

er

er与英语单词“younger”中“er”的发音基本相同。

The pronunciation of “er” is similar to that of “er” in English word “younger”.

拼音	er
英语	younger

提示 Be aware

隔音符号 Dividing mark

ɑ、o、e开头的音节连接在其他音节后面时，为了使音节界限清楚，不会混淆，要用隔音符号“’”隔开。如nǚ' ér（女儿 daughter）。

The “ ’ ” is to separate two neighboring syllables when the second syllable begins with “ɑ, o, e”, for example, nǚ' ér (daughter).

随堂练 Classroom exercises

1. 将下面的韵母写成独立的音节。Respell the finals below as independent syllables.

ian — ing — iong — uo — uɑi —

ueng — üe — üɑn — ün —

2. 将下面的声母、韵母拼合起来。Combine the following initials and finals.

d + iou → h + uei → l + iou → k + uen →

d + uei → t + uen → n + iou → g + uei →

3. 读一读下面的音节。Read the following syllables.

biǎo	niǎo	niú	tiān
liǎn	língtīng	húdié	miàntiáo
hǎibiān	sēnlín	qiántiān	zuótiān
jīntiān	míngtiān	hòutiān	

4. 听录音并跟读。Read after the recording.

píng'ān	kě'ài	xī'ān	hǎi'ōu	pí'ǎo
lián'ǒu	yú'é	dàng'àn	shí'èr	fāng'àn

5. 听录音并跟读，注意每组韵母的不同。Read after the recording, and pay attention to the difference within each pair.

liǎn	liǎng
duò	dòu
wèn	wèng
gòu	guò

lüè	liè
mín	míng
tòu	tuò

wán	wáng
lòu	luò
lù	lǜ

课堂活动 Activities

听音举牌：学生分为两个小组，每组分给一套拼音卡，每个学生手中有若干张拼音卡，听到老师的发音后，持有相应卡片的小组成员迅速举牌。

Raise the Pinyin cards according to the teacher's pronunciation: Divide the class into two groups and give each group a set of Pinyin cards, each students with several at hand. On hearing the teacher's pronunciation, the group members who have the corresponding cards are supposed to raise them up as quickly as possible.

二 声母 | Initials

j q x

z c s

zh ch
sh r

1 发音与英语一致的声母 The initials sharing the same pronunciation with their English "counterparts"

拼音	s
英语	stop

随堂练 Classroom exercises

听录音并跟读。Read after the recording.

sì	sǎng	sēn	sú	sān	sǎo	sōu
sè	sòng	sēng	sǎ	sāi		

2 发音与英语能基本对应（≠完全对应）的声母 The initials approximately corresponding to their English "counterparts"

拼音	z	c
英语	kids	cats

提示 Be aware

z、c

英语“kids”发音中的[dz]，发音时声带应振动，但汉语中z和c发音时声带都不振动。z是不送气音，发z时，呼出气流较弱，而c是送气音，发c时，呼出气流较强。z和c的发音方法如下图所示：

The sound [dz] in the English word “kids” is produced with vibration of the vocal cord, but the Chinese “z” and “c” are both without the vibration. “z” is unaspirated consonant, which is pronounced with very weak breath; while “c” is aspirated consonant with stronger breath. The tongue positions of “z” and “c” are shown below:

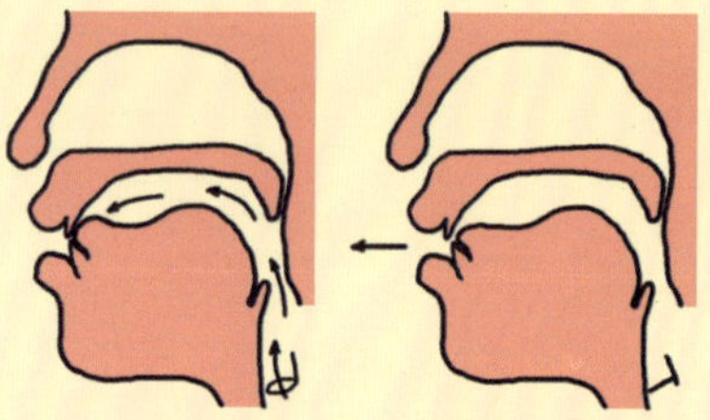

z的舌位图
The tongue position of “z”

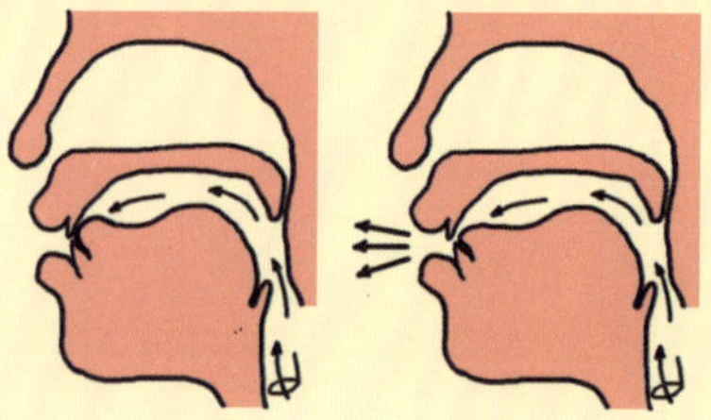

c的舌位图
The tongue position of “c”

随 堂 练
Classroom exercises

1. 听录音并跟读。Read after the recording.

zì　cí　sì　suī　sǔn　sè　zǔ　zé　cān　céng

2. 听老师的发音，写下声母，并跟读。Listen to the teacher, write down the initials, and read after the teacher.

__ài　__āo　__én　__ǎn　__òng　__áng
__ū　__ùn　__uī　__èng　__uò　__uàn

课堂活动 Activities

语音抢答：听老师的发音，抢答老师所说的是z、c、s 3个声母中的哪一个。

Listen to the teacher and point out the one pronounced by the teacher from the 3 initials “z, c, s”— the faster, the better.

3 发音较特殊的声母 The initials with special pronunciation

j q x zh ch sh r

j有些像英语“jeep”中的“j”；q有些像英语“cheap”中的“ch”；x有些像英语“she”中的“sh”。

“j” is, to some degree, pronounced like “j” in the English word “jeep”; “q” like “ch” in “cheap”; “x” like “sh” in “she”.

但与英语不同的是，发这三个音时，舌尖都要略微往前，顶住下齿背，舌面前部上贴硬腭，嘴唇向后平展。

However, unlike their English “counterparts”, these three initials are produced with the tip of the tongue forward against the back of the lower teeth, the front part of the tongue very close to the hard palate, and lips drawn wide and backwards.

发j的时候，舌面前部先抵住硬腭，再松开一条窄缝。

发q的部位与j相同，只是应用力送气。

发x的部位与j、q一样，只是舌面和硬腭并不接触，中间形成一条窄缝。

When pronouncing “j”, raise the front of the tongue against the hard palate first, and then loose to a narrow gap. “q” shares the same tongue position with “j”, but should be aspirated with strong breath. The tongue position of “x” is the same as “j” and “q”. The only difference is that when pronouncing “x”, the tip of the tongue never touches the hard palate, always with a thin gap in between.

zh有些像英语“jump”中的“j”；ch有些像英语“china”中的“ch”；sh有些像英语“shy”中的“sh”；r有些像英语“right”中的“r”。

“zh” is, to some degree, pronounced like “j” in the English word “jump”; “ch” like “ch” in “china”; “sh” like “sh” in “shy”; and “r” like “r” in “right”.

但与英语不同的是，这四个音的舌尖都要向上翘起，接近上齿龈后边的硬腭部位。

But, different from English, these four initials are produced with the tip of the tongue upward close to the hard palate near upper gum.

发zh的时候，舌尖先抵住硬腭，再往后卷。

发ch的部位与zh一样，只是应用力送气。

发sh的部位与zh、ch一样，只是舌尖和硬腭并不接触，中间形成一条窄缝。

“zh” starts with the tongue touching the hard palate and then curls the tongue back. “ch” shares the same tongue position with “zh”, but should be aspirated with strong breath. The tongue position of “sh” is the same as “zh” and “ch”. The only difference is that when pronouncing “sh”, the tip of the tongue never touches the hard palate, always with a thin gap in between.

▶ 提示 Be aware

① z、zh、j不送气（呼出气流较弱），c、ch、q送气（呼出气流较强）。

“z, zh, j” are unaspirated consonants, which are pronounced with very weak breath; while “c, ch, q” are aspirated ones with stronger breath.

不送气	z	zh	j	unaspirated
送气	c	ch	q	aspirated

② 发z、c、s时，舌尖要靠前（抵住或接近上齿背），不要翘起；发zh、ch、sh时，舌尖要靠后一些（抵住或接近硬腭前部），并且翘起来。

When pronouncing “z, c, s”, the tip of the tongue is placed forward (touching against or approaching the back of the upper teeth), and the tongue isn't curled. When pronouncing "zh, ch, sh", the tip of the tongue is placed backward (touching against or approaching the front part of the hard palate) and then the tongue is curled back.

③ zi、ci、si和zhi、chi、shi、ri中的韵母不能读成[i]。zi、ci、si的韵母是舌尖前音[ɿ]，zhi、chi、shi、ri的韵母是舌尖后音[ʅ]。

The finals in "zi, ci, si" and "zhi, chi, shi, ri" can not be pronounced as [i]. The finals in "zi, ci, si" are read as [ɿ], which is pronounced with the tip of the tongue approaching the back of the teeth; while the finals in "zhi, chi, shi, ri" are read as [ʅ], which is pronounced with the tip of the tongue approaching the front part of the hard palate.

④ z、c、s和zh、ch、sh、r不与单韵母ü或以i、ü开头的复韵母相拼。

"z, c, s" and "zh, ch, sh, r" are not combined with "ü", or compound finals which begin with "i, ü".

⑤ ju、qu、xu

因为j、q、x只与i、ü或以i、ü开头的韵母相拼，不与u或以u开头的韵母相拼。所以，当j、q、x跟ü及以ü开头的韵母拼合时，ü上的两点省略。如：

When "j, q, x" are followed by "ü", the dots on top of the "ü" are removed, because "j, q, x" are never followed by "u". But it is still pronounced as "ü", not "u". For example:

j + ü → ju　　q + üe → que　　x + üan → xuan

随堂练
Classroom exercises

1. 将下面的声母、韵母拼合起来。Combine the initials and finals below.

j + üan →　　l + üe →　　q + ün →　　x + üan →

2. 听录音并跟读。Read after the recording.

jí qí xí

jiān qiān xiān

jiāng qiāng xiāng

jǔ qǔ xǔ

juān quān xuān

jūn qūn xūn

zhì chì shì rì

zhǎn chǎn shǎn rǎn

zhàng chàng shàng ràng

zhǔ chǔ shǔ rǔ

zhuān chuān shuān

zhǔn chǔn shǔn

3. 辨别对错。指出老师的发音是对的还是错的，如果是错的，请说出正确的发音。

True/False. Tell true or false about the teacher's pronunciation and correct the wrong ones.

zhī	chè	qǐ	xì	jǐ
shā	ruò	zòu	cái	sū

4. 听老师的发音，标出你听到的拼音。Listen to the teacher and mark the Pinyin you hear.

jí —— qí

zhù —— chù

zá —— zhá

zēng —— zhēng —— jīng

cī —— chī —— qī

sù —— shù —— xù

课堂活动 Activities

语音抢答：听老师的发音，抢答老师说的是j、q、x、z、c、s、zh、ch、sh、r 等声母中的哪一个。

Listen to the teacher and point out the one pronounced by the teacher from the 7 initials "j, q, x, z, c, s, zh, ch, sh, r" — the faster, the better.

三　声调 | Tones

1　标调规则（2）Rules for marking tones (II)

第 课讲到，声调符号要标在元音上，当一个音节有两个或两个以上的元音时，要标在开口度大的元音上。对于本课所学韵母来说，当开头的i、u、ü后有其他元音时，声调符号要标在其他元音上，如xiè、jué，如果后面没有其他元音，就标在i、u、ü上，如dùn、tíng。但如果韵母是iu或ui，调号要标在后一个元音上，如xiū、ruǐ。

As is mentioned in Lesson 1, the tone mark always falls on a vowel of the syllable. When there are two or more vowels in one final, the tone mark falls on top of the vowel with bigger opening. For what we learned in this lesson, when "i, u, ü" come before other vowels, the tone mark is on top of the following vowel, such as "xiè, jué". If there are no other vowels following, "i, u, ü" carries the tone mark, such as "dùn, tíng". In case the compound final is "iu，ui", the tone is always marked on top of the latter vowel, like "xiū, ruǐ" .

随堂练 Classroom exercises

听录音，标声调。Listen to the recording and mark the tones.

jia	hua	wan	quan	liu	dui	wen	qian
qing	yue	luo	hou	tun	liang	diu	tui
tai	pao	biao	meng				

四　练习 | Exercises

1. 唱四声。Read aloud the four tones.

cān	cán	căn	càn
shēn	shén	shĕn	shèn
chāng	cháng	chăng	chàng
pēng	péng	pĕng	pèng
tōng	tóng	tŏng	tòng

2. 辨音。Pronunciation differentiation.

(1) zū — cū　　jǔ — qǔ　　zhù — chù

(2) zǎo — zhǎo　　cóng — chóng　　sēn — shēn　　lè — rè

(3) qián — qiáng　　jīn — jīng　　zhěn — zhěng

(4) zǒu — zuǒ　　guò — gòu　　luó — lóu　　shōu — shuō

zhòu — chòu — shòu — ròu　　zhuō — chuō — shuō

(5) duī — diū　　cuī — qiū　　liǔ — ruǐ　　shuì — xiù

3. 辨调。Tone differentiation.

dàyú — dàyǔ	xiǎojié — xiǎojiě
běijīng — bèijǐng	qǐngwèn — qīngwěn
jiàoshī — jiàoshì	měiyuán — méiyuán
wúshù — wǔshù	shuìjiào — shuǐjiǎo
mǎibù — màibù	dàolǐ — dàolì

4. 朗读下列双音节词语。Read the following bi-syllablic words.

fāyīn	kāixīn	sījī	dōngtiān
wēnróu	jīnnián	sānshí	kāimén
hēshuǐ	kāishǐ	shēntǐ	jīchǎng
fāxiàn	shēngqì	chīfàn	gōngzuò

5. 读短句。Read the short sentences aloud.

Yīyuàn hěn yuǎn. The hospital is very far.

Yán hěn xián. The salt is very salty.

Wǒ xiǎng nǐ. I miss you.

Tāng hěn tàng. The soup is very hot.

Táng hěn tián. The sugar is very sweet.

Wǒ xǐhuan hē tāng, yě xǐhuan chī táng. I like to drink soup. I also like to eat sugar.

6. 听录音填写声母，然后跟读。Listen to the recording, fill in the initials, and read aloud.

___iā	___ù	___ǎng	___ēn	___ī	___ì
___iào	___ué	___ún	___iě	___uī	___uàn
___uǎn	___ǔn	___ǔ	___ián	___iǒng	___iāng

7. 听录音填写韵母和声调，然后跟读。Listen to the recording, fill in the finals and tones, and read aloud.

x___	x___	x___	j___	j___	j___
q___	q___	q___	h___	d___	k___
d___	zh___	sh___	ch___	d___	l___

五 现学现用 | Survival Chinese

文化知识

Chinese ABC

数字

Number

Some numbers indicate luck or fates in Chinese culture. For instance,"4(sì)" sounds similar to "死(sǐ)" which means "death", so many people would try to avoid this number in their life. "8(bā)" sounds like "发(fā)", which means "to make a fortune". Therefore, the cellphone numbers or car plates with one or more "8" are popular and sell for a better price. "6(liù)" is considered as a lucky number to indicate "things going smoothly". And "9(jiǔ)" means "everlasting" and is adored by couples. For this reason, on the Valentine's Day, roses are usually sold in a bunch of 9 or 99, or even 999.

1	2	3	4	5	6	7	8	9	10
yī	èr	sān	sì	wǔ	liù	qī	bā	jiǔ	shí
one	two	three	four	five	six	seven	eight	nine	ten

汉语拼音声母表
Chinese Initials

b[p]	p[p‘]	m[m]	f[f]	d[t]	t[t‘]	n[n]	l[l]
g[k]	k[k‘]	h[x]		j[tɕ]	q[tɕ‘]	x[ɕ]	
zh[tʂ]	ch[tʂ‘]	sh[ʂ]	r[ʐ]	z[ts]	c[ts‘]	s[s]	

汉语拼音韵母表
Chinese Finals

	i [i] 衣	u [u] 乌	ü [y] 迂
a [A] 啊	ia [iA] 呀	ua [uA] 蛙	
o [o] 喔		uo [uo] 窝	
e [ɣ] 鹅	ie [iɛ] 耶		üe [yɛ] 约
ai [ai] 哀		uai [uai] 歪	
ei [ei] 欸		uei [uei] 威	
ao [ɑu] 熬	iao [iɑu] 腰		
ou [ou] 欧	iou [iou] 忧		
an [an] 安	ian [iɛn] 烟	uan [uan] 弯	üan [yɛn] 冤
en [ən] 恩	in [in] 因	uen [uən] 温	ün [yn] 晕
ang [ɑŋ] 昂	iang [iɑŋ] 央	uang [uɑŋ] 汪	
eng [əŋ] 亨的韵母	ing [iŋ] 英	ueng [uəŋ] 翁	
ong [uŋ] 轰的韵母	iong [yŋ] 雍		

第三课 Lesson 3

汉字（一）Characters (I)

学习要点

1 汉字：人、日、月、目、口、山、水、大、天、火 的意义及写法

2 汉字基本笔画

3 汉字基本笔顺

4 语音：三声变调

一 猜字义，学汉字

Guess the meanings and learn characters

先看左边的图和象形符号，猜猜它们的意思，再看右边，学习汉字。

Look at the pictures and pictographs on the left, guess their meanings, and then read the right side to learn the characters.

人

人 rén	*n.* people; person

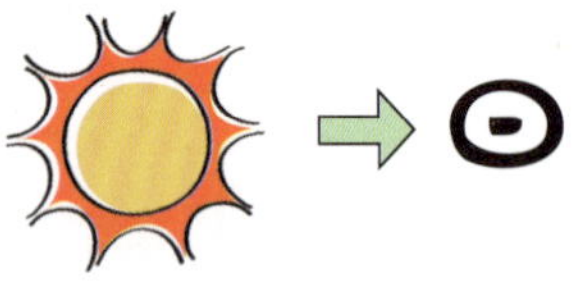

日

日 rì	*n.* sun

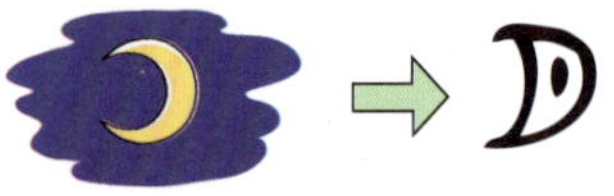

月

月 yuè	*n.* moon

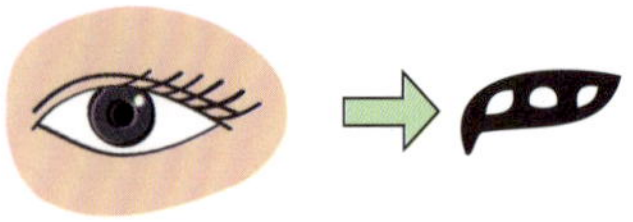

目

目 mù	*n.* eye

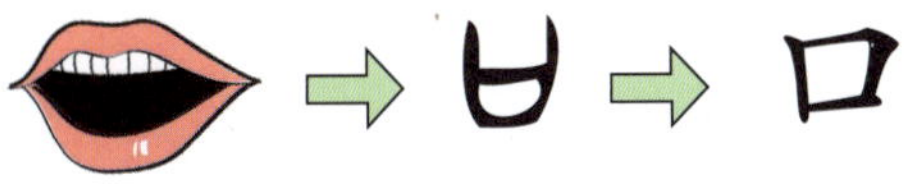

口 kǒu *n.* mouth

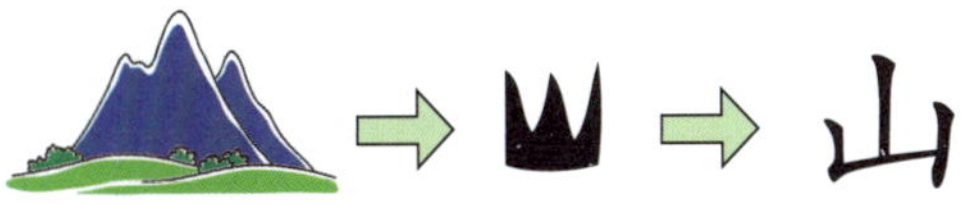

山 shān *n.* mountain;hill

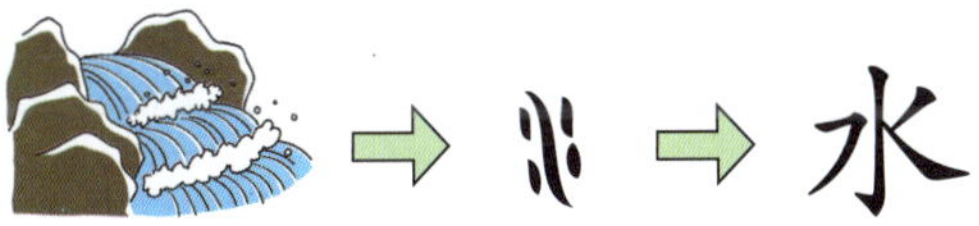

水 shuǐ *n.* water

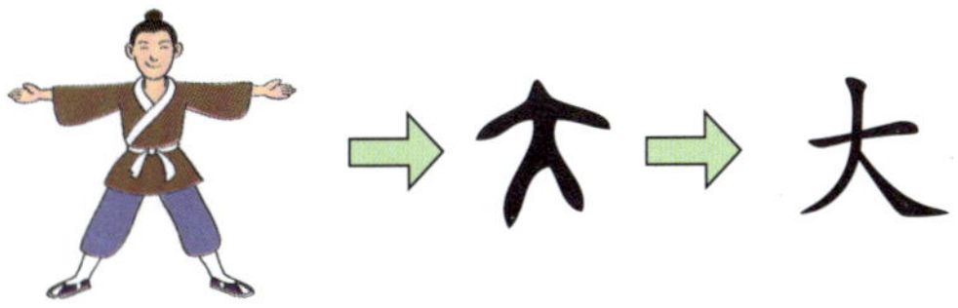

大 dà *adj.* big

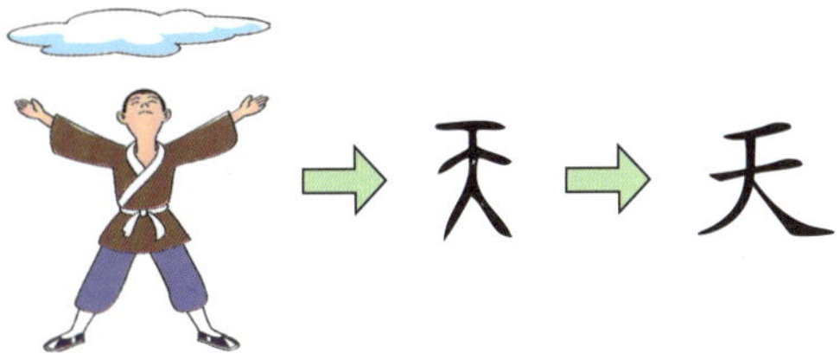

天 tiān *n.* sky

Tips: The sky is above man.

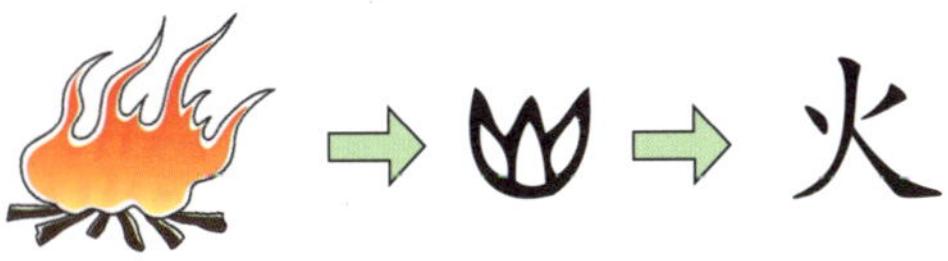

火 huǒ *n.* fire

二 汉字基本笔画 | Basic strokes

Basic strokes		Names in Pinyin	Examples
1.	丶	diǎn	火
2.	一	héng	大 天 口 目
3.	丨	shù	山 口 日 目
4.	丿	piě	人 大 天 月
5.	㇏	nà	人 大 天 水
6.	㇀	tí	氵
7.	㇕	héngzhé	口 日 目
8.	㇆	héngzhégōu	月
9.	㇇	héngpiě	水
10.	㇄	shùzhé	山
11.	亅	shùgōu	水

三 汉字基本笔顺 | Stroke order

1. 从左到右 From left to right

人 丿 → 人

火 丶 → 丷 → 少 → 火

2. 从上到下 From top to bottom

天 一 → 二 → チ → 天

3. 先横后竖 Horizontal before vertical

大 一 → ナ → 大

4. 从外到内 From outside to inside

月 丿 → 冂 → 月 → 月

5. 先中间后两边 Middle before two sides

山 丨 → 山 → 山

水 亅 → 力 → 水 → 水

6. 从外到内后封口 Inside before closing

日 丨 → 冂 → 日 → 日

目 丨 → 冂 → 月 → 月 → 目

汉字练习 Character exercises

1. 写汉字，注意笔画笔顺。Write the following characters and pay attention to the stroke order.

人	丿	人			
日	丨	冂	月	日	
月	丿	月	月	月	
目	丨	冂	月	月	目
口	丨	冂	口		

山	丨	山	山		
水	亅	刁	水	水	
大	一	ナ	大		
天	一	二	チ	天	
火	丶	丷	火	火	

2. 根据所学内容写出下列字符和图画所对应的现代汉字。Write down the modern characters corresponding to the following pictographs and pictures.

3. 根据笔画数为下列汉字归类。Classify the characters according to the number of strokes.

人　大　天　火　口　日　月　目　山　水

2 strokes

3 strokes

4 strokes

5 strokes

4. 将汉字与其相对应的读音连起来。Match the characters with their Pinyin.

大	tiān
火	rén
天	dà
人	huǒ
山	shān

日	yuè
口	rì
月	mù
目	kǒu
水	shuǐ

5. 从本课所学的汉字中，找出带有下面笔画的汉字。Find out the characters learned in this lesson that are with the following strokes.

6. 看字卡（或板书），找找这几个字的不同。Look at the character cards (or characters on the blackboard), and find the difference in each group.

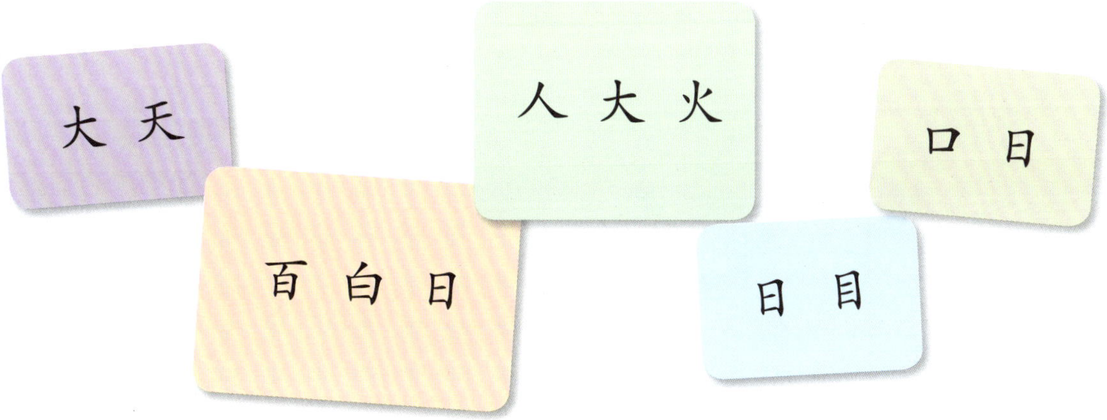

课堂活动 Activities

1. 听音抢字卡：老师把汉字卡片悬挂在黑板上，学生分成两组，找出与老师发音相符合的字卡，抢到的字卡多的一组获胜。

   Card picking competition: The class is divided into two groups and compete for picking the character cards on the blackboard which match the teacher's pronunciation. The group with more cards wins.

2. 补全汉字：老师在黑板上写出笔画残缺的汉字，由学生补全该汉字。

   Complete the characters: The teacher writes characters with some strokes missing on the blackboard, and asks students to complete them.

四 语音 | Phonetics

三声变调 Third-tone sandhi

两个三声音节相连，前一个三声要读成二声，但在写拼音时，仍然标为三声。

If two third-tone syllables are uttered in succession, the first third-tone syllable is pronounced as the second tone. But when writing the Pinyin, we don't change the tone mark from the third to the second.

语音练习 Phonetic exercises

1. 听录音并跟读。Read after the recording.

shuǐguǒ	xǐlǐ	fǔdǎo	měihǎo	chǐrǔ
qǔshě	kěyǐ	yǔfǎ	běihǎi	wǔbǎi
shuǐcǎo	xǐzǎo	liǎojiě	fǎngǎn	gǎnxiǎng
yǔsǎn	yǎnjiǎng	lǎohǔ	lǎoshǔ	wǔdǎo

2. 听录音，标出每个音节的声调。Listen to the recording and mark the tone of each syllable.

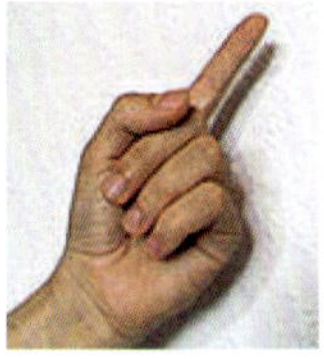
yi
一

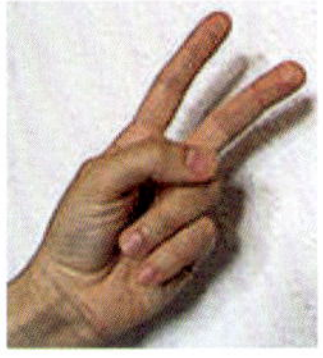
er
二

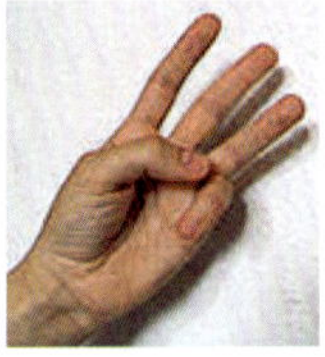
san
三

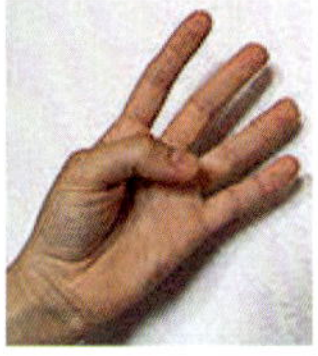
si
四

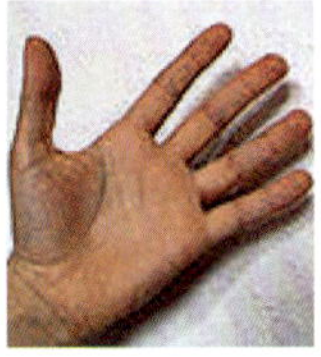
wu
五

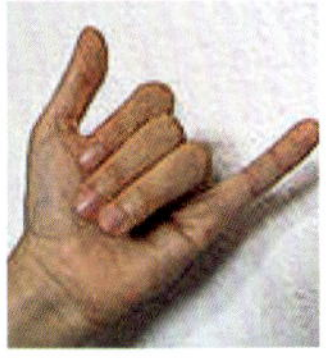
liu
六

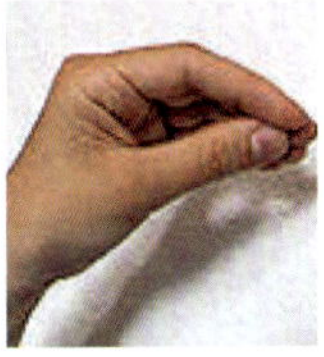
qi
七

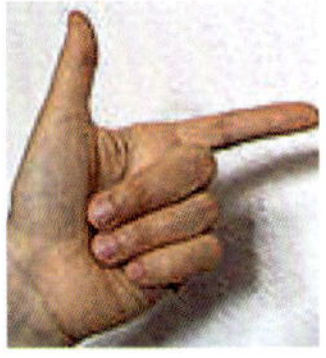
ba
八

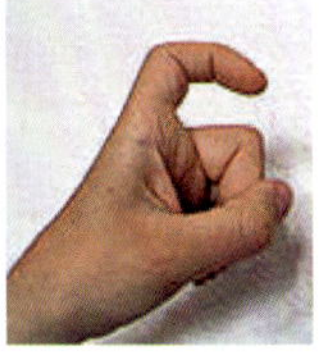
jiu
九

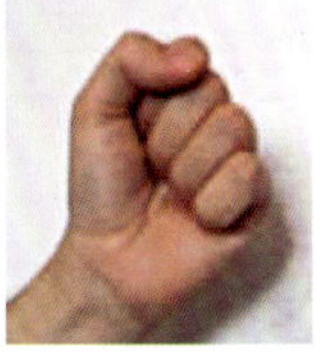
shi
十

3. 听录音填写声母。Listen to the recording and fill in the initials.

___ōng___uó　　___ěi___īng　　___àng___ǎi　　___uǎng___ōu

___ī___ān　　___ué___iào　　___iào___ì　　___ān___īng

___ú___ū___uǎn　　___èi___ēng___iān

4. 听录音填写韵母和声调。Listen to the recording and fill in the finals and tones.

z_____y_____　　k_____sh_____　　r_____l_____　　sh_____w_____

m_____t_____　　w_____q_____　　y_____y_____　　p_____b_____

d_____l_____　　y_____d_____

5. 看拼音，读一读下列词语，查查它们的意思。Read the following words by Pinyin and try to find out their meanings in the dictionary.

réncái	gōngrén	shāngrén	jiārén	dàren	dàxué
人才	工人	商人	家人	大人	大学
zhǎngdà	Běidà	tiānkōng	tiānqì	báitiān	jīntiān
长大	北大	天空	天气	白天	今天
dàhuǒ	shuǐhuǒ	mièhuǒ	huǒshān	kǒuyǔ	kǒuhóng
大火	水火	灭火	火山	口语	口红
rénkǒu	ménkǒu	rìyǔ	rìlì	shēngrì	jiérì
人口	门口	日语	日历	生日	节日
yuèguāng	yuèbing	yīyuè	sānyuè	mùdì	mùlù
月光	月饼	一月	三月	目的	目录
jiémù	qǔmù	shānshuǐ	shānqū	dàshān	míngshān
节目	曲目	山水	山区	大山	名山
shuǐlì	shuǐtǔ	zìláishuǐ	kuàngquánshuǐ		
水利	水土	自来水	矿泉水		

课堂活动 Activities

1. 认读字卡，写出拼音：老师举起本课所学汉字的字卡，要求学生在黑板上写出拼音。

   Read character cards and write Pinyin: The teacher raises the character cards of this lesson and asks students to write down the Pinyin on the blackboard.

2. 拼写比赛：老师事先准备好两张写有相同数量拼音的卡片，将学生分为两组，每组由一位同学发音，另一位同学根据其发音在黑板上写出拼音，若写对则可以继续写下一个音，若写错则该组换人，最终使用人数少的一组获胜。

   Pinyin competition: The teacher prepares two cards with the same amount of Pinyin and divides the whole class into two groups. One student in each group reads the Pinyin on the card aloud, and another student from the same group transcribes what he/she hears into Pinyin on the blackboard. The one who does correct transcription continues, while the one who makes mistakes should be substituted by another group member. The group with fewer transcribers wins.

五 现学现用 | Survival Chinese

1. 熟读下列句子。Read the following sentences over.

1）Hěn hǎo! Very good.
2）Qǐng gēn wǒ dú. Please read after me.
3）Wǒ tīng bù dǒng. I heard it, but I don't understand.
4）Wǒ bù zhīdào. I don't know.
5）Qǐng zài shuō yí cì. Please say it again.
6）"……" shì shénme yìsi? What does "…" mean?

2. 请将图中人物说的话用汉语再说一遍。Interpret what the people in the pictures say into Chinese.

文化知识
Chinese ABC

汉字带来的灵感
Inspiration Brought by Chinese Characters

jīng

Chinese characters play an important role in the life of the Chinese. As the written symbol of the language, a character also incarnates the pronunciation and the meaning and sparkles the Chinese people's inspiration in art. China's calligraphy is a style of art based on the artistic elements in the writing of the Chinese characters. Take the badge of the 2008 Olympic Games as an example. In the traditional Chinese seal, there is the character "京" (from "北京 Beijing") in the ancient form. Inspired by pictographs and calligraphy, the designer developed "京" into the shape of a dancing human figure. By doing that, the ancient Chinese art and the modern Olympic spirit were combined in one image, delivering the message to the world that "Beijing is dancing for the Olympics."

第四课 Lesson 4 汉字（二）Characters (2)

学习要点

1 汉字：木、林、本、上、下、明、相、泪、文、白、百、小、少的意义及写法

2 语音：轻声

一 猜字义，学汉字

Guess the meanings and learn characters

先看左边的图和象形符号，猜猜它们的意思，再看右边，学习汉字。

Look at the pictures and pictographs on the left, guess their meanings, and then read the right side to learn the characters.

→ 木

木 mù	一	十	才	木	
	n. tree; wood				

→ 林

林 lín	一	十	才	木	林
	n. woods; forest				

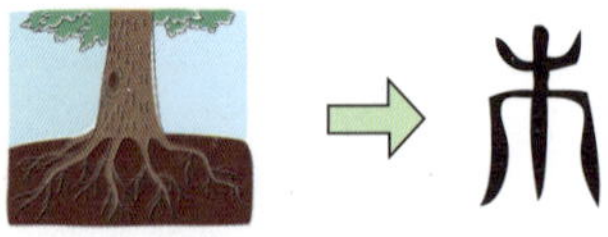
→ 本

本 běn	一	十	才	木	本
	n. root of a plant				

Tips: A short horizontal stroke going across the lower part of the character “木” indicates “the root of a plant”.

→ 上

上 shàng	丨	卜	上		
	n./v. on; above; upward				

→ 下

下 xià	一	丅	下		
	n./v. below; under; downward				

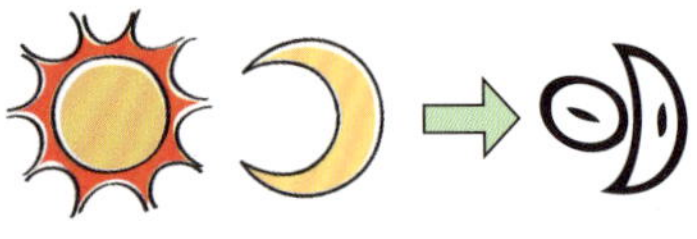
→ 明

明 míng	丨	日	明		
	adj. bright				

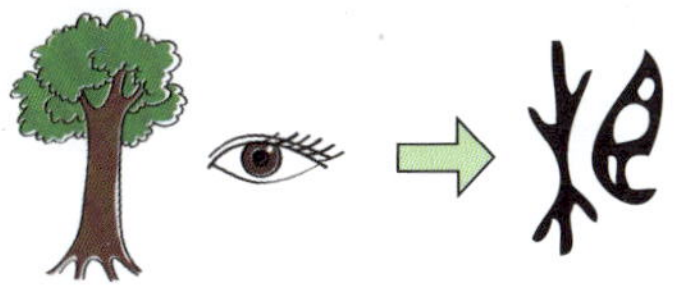
→ 相

相 xiàng 一 木 相 *v.* to observe and judge

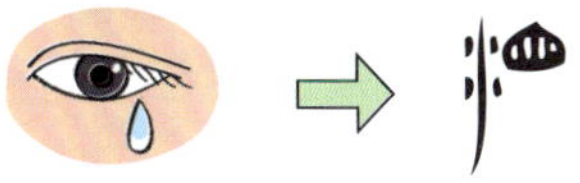
→ 泪

泪 lèi 丶 丶 氵 泪 *n.* tear

→ 文

文 wén 丶 亠 ナ 文 *n.* character; writing

以下图片并不显示汉字的本义，仅用于帮助记忆汉字字形。

The pictures below don't show the original meanings of the characters, but they might help you to remember the characters.

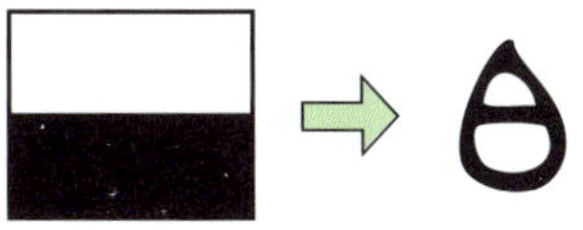
→ 白

白 bái ノ 丨 白 白 白 *adj.* white

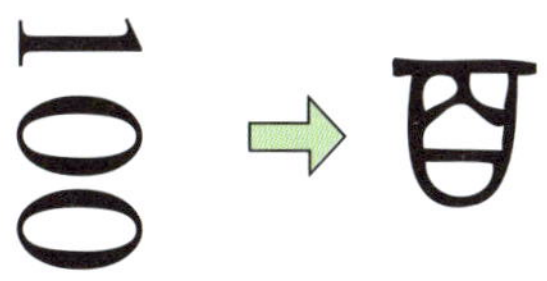

→ 百

百 bǎi 一 百 *num.* hundred

→ 小

小 xiǎo 亅 小 小 *adj.* small; little

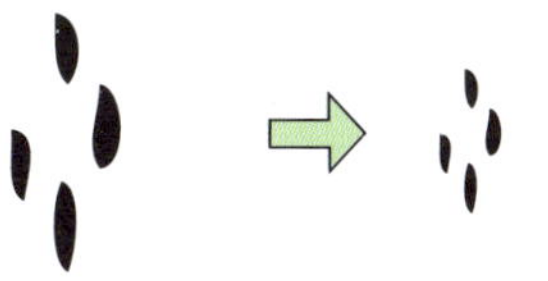
→ 少

少 shǎo 丨 小 小 少 *adj.* few; little

汉字练习 Character exercises

1. 写汉字，注意笔画笔顺。Write the following characters and pay attention to the stroke order.

木	一	十	才	木						
林	一	十	才	木	木	村	材	林		
本	一	十	才	木	本					
上	丨	卜	上							
下	一	丅	下							
明	丨	冂	月	日	日丿	明	明	明		
相	一	十	才	木	木丨	机	相	相	相	
泪	丶	冫	氵	氵丨	汩	泪	泪	泪		
文	丶	亠	方	文						
白	丿	亻	白	白	白					

百	一	丆	丆	丙	百	百				
小	亅	亅	小							
少	丨	丨	小	少						

2. 根据所学内容写出下列字符和图画所对应的现代汉字。Write down the modern characters corresponding to the following pictographs and pictures.

3. 根据笔画数为下列汉字归类。Classify the characters according to the number of strokes.

文 木 林 本 相 泪 小 少 明 白 上 下 百

3 strokes

4 strokes

5 strokes

6 strokes

8 strokes

9 strokes

4. 将汉字与其相对应的读音连起来。Match the characters with their Pinyin.

木	shàng
白	xiǎo
小	mù
上	bái

本	běn
百	shǎo
少	xià
下	bǎi

明	xiàng
相	wén
文	míng
林	lèi
泪	lín

5. 看字卡（或板书），找找这几个字的不同。Look at the character cards (or characters on the blackboard), and find the difference in each group.

木 本

文 大 天

小 少

上 下

泪 相

课堂活动 Activities

1. 听音抢字卡：老师把汉字卡片悬挂在黑板上，学生分成两组，找出与老师发音相符合的字卡，抢到的字卡多的一组获胜。

   Card picking competition: The class is divided into two groups and compete for picking the character cards on the blackboard which match the teacher's pronunciation. The group with more cards wins.

2. 补全汉字：老师在黑板上写出笔画残缺的汉字，由学生补全该汉字。

   Complete the characters: The teacher writes characters with some strokes missing on the blackboard, and asks students to complete them.

二 语音 | Phonetics

轻声 Neutral tone

普通话里有一些音节读得又短又轻，叫做轻声。书写时轻声不标调号。例如：

In Mandarin, some syllables are both short and light, which are named neutral tone. In writing, a neutral-tone syllable carries no tone mark. For example:

bàba（爸爸 father）
māma（妈妈 mother）
wǒmen（我们 we; us）
tāmen（他们 they; them）
shénme（什么 what）
míngzi（名字 name）
Hǎo ma?（好吗? OK?）
Nǐ ne?（你呢? How about you?/ And you?）

随堂练 Classroom exercises

听录音并跟读。Read after the recording.

dōngxi	línzi	běnshi	mùtou	māma	míngzi
wǎnshang	dìfang	péngyou	shíhou	zǎoshang	xièxie

语音练习 Phonetic exercises

1. 在空白处写出听到的拼音，了解一下中国人的家庭关系。Write down the Pinyin in the blanks according to what you hear and learn about the family relationship of Chinese people.

2. 听录音，标出第一个音节的声调。Listen to the recording and mark the tone of the first syllable in each word.

baba	mama	gege	jiejie	didi	meimei
erzi	panzi	kuaizi	zhen de	hao de	ni de
women	nimen	lai ba	zou ba	chile	shuile
toufa	dongxi	name	yuan ma	keqi	xiexie

3. 听录音填空。Fill in the blanks according to the recording.

mù______	______běn	bái______	èr______
______shuō	shào______	shàng______	______qu
míng______	______lín	xiàng______	______lèi
ér______	______zi	______tou	zhěn______
______duo	péng______	______sheng	______men

4. 听录音，写句子。Listen to the recording and write down the sentences in Pinyin.

1）________________________ Please read after me.

2）________________________ Please listen to me.

3）________________________ Please say it again.

4）________________________ If you have questions, please ask me.

5. 看拼音，读一读下列词语，查查它们的意思。Read the following words by Pinyin and try to find out their meanings in the dictionary.

mùcái 木材	shùmù 树木	běnlái 本来	gēnběn 根本	báitiān 白天	báisè 白色	hēibái 黑白
bǎihuò 百货	bǎinián 百年	bànbǎi 半百	xiǎoshì 小事	dàxiǎo 大小	shǎojiàn 少见	duōshǎo 多少
bù shǎo 不少	shànglái 上来	shàngqù 上去	shàng chē 上车	shàng shān 上山	xiàlái 下来	xiàqù 下去
xià chē 下车	xià shān 下山	shān shàng 山上	shān xià 山下	guāngmíng 光明	míngliàng 明亮	míngtiān 明天
míngnián 明年	shùlín 树林	sēnlín 森林	xiàngjī 相机	zhàoxiàng 照相	lèishuǐ 泪水	yǎnlèi 眼泪
wénzì 文字	wénhuà 文化	Zhōngwén 中文	Yīngwén 英文			

三 现学现用 | Survival Chinese

1. 熟读下列句子。Read the following sentences over.

1）"……" Zhōngwén zěnme shuō? — How do you say "…" in Chinese?

2）Zhège zì zěnme dú? — How do you pronounce this character?

3）Qǐng màn yìdiǎnr. — Please be a little slower./ Slowly, please.

4）Qǐng kuài yìdiǎnr. — Please be a little faster./ Hurry up!

5）Qǐng gàosu wǒ... — Please kindly tell me.../Excuse me...

2. 请将图中人物说的话用汉语再说一遍。Interpret what the people in the pictures say into Chinese.

文化知识
Chinese ABC

汉字的构成（一）

The Formation of Chinese Characters (I)

Chinese characters can be divided into four categories according to their formation: pictographic characters (象形字), self-explanatory characters (指事字), associative compounds (会意字) and pictophonetic characters (形声字).

1 象形字 Pictographic characters

Some Chinese characters evolved from pictures, such as "人，口，日，月，目，山，水", are called pictographic characters. But pictographic characters comprise only a very small proportion, since many things are difficult to be depicted by pictures.

2 指事字 Self-explanatory characters

Self-explanatory characters are formed by adding simple and abstract signs to pictographic characters. For example, "本" is formed by adding a horizontal stroke at the lower part of "木"; "上" and "下" are formed by adding signs above or below the stroke "一".

第五课 Lesson 5

汉字（三）Characters (3)

学习要点

1 汉字：米、来、刀、力、田、手、心、女、子、门、好、男、问、想的意义及写法

2 汉字基本结构

3 语音：儿化

一 猜字义，学汉字

Guess the meanings and learn characters

先看左边的图和象形符号，猜猜它们的意思，再看右边，学习汉字。

Look at the pictures and pictographs on the left, guess their meanings, and then read the right side to learn the characters.

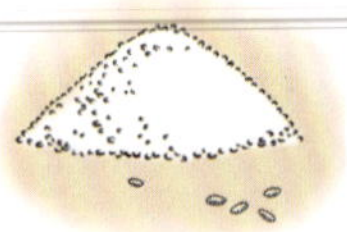 →  → 米

米 mǐ	*n.* rice

 →  → 来

来 lái	*v.* to come

Tips: "来" originally means "wheat", but it was borrowed to mean "to come".

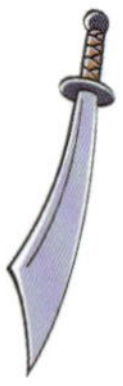 →  → 刀

刀 dāo	*n.* knife

 →  → 力

力 lì	*n.* force; power; strength

 →  → 田

田 tián	*n.* field; farmland

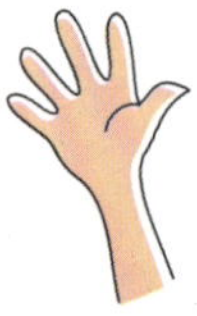 →  → 手

手 shǒu	*n.* hand

 →  → 心

心 xīn	丶	心	心	心	
	n. heart				

 →  → 女

女 nǚ	く	女	女		
	n. female; woman				

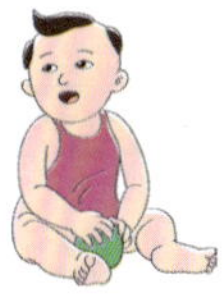 →  → 子

子 zǐ	㇇	了	子		
	n. son; child				

 →  → 门

门 mén	丶	丶丨	门		
	n. door; gate				

 →  → 好

好 hǎo	く	女	女	女㇇	好
	adj. good; nice; well				

 →  → 男

男 nán	丨	冂	田	男	男
	n. male; man				

 →  → 问

问 wèn	丶	丶丨	门	门	问
	v. to ask				

 →  → 想

想 xiǎng	木	木	相	相	想
	v. to think				

二 汉字基本结构

Basic structures of Chinese characters

1. 

独体字 Single component

Only one part

人、大、女、力、米、手、心、子、门

2. 

上下结构 Top-bottom

One part on the top and the other at the bottom

男、想

3. 

左右结构 Left-right

One part on the left and the other on the right

林、明、好

4. 

包围结构（左、上、右三面） Surrounding (three-sided)

One part surrounding on three sides with only the bottom open

问

汉字练习 Character exercises

1. 写汉字，注意笔画笔顺。Write the following characters and pay attention to the stroke order.

米	丶	丷	丷	半	米	米								
来	一	丆	丆	平	平	来	来							
刀	𠃌	刀												

力	㇆	力											
田	丨	冂	冂	用	田								
手	丿	二	三	手									
心	丶	心	心	心									
女	𡿨	女	女										
子	㇇	了	子										
门	丶	门	门										
好	𡿨	女	女	好	好	好							
男	丨	冂	日	田	田	男	男						
问	丶	门	门	问	问	问							
想	一	十	木	木	相	相	相	相	相	相	想	想	想

2. 根据所学内容写出下列字符和图画所对应的现代汉字。Write down the modern characters corresponding to the following pictographs and pictures.

3. 根据笔画数为下列汉字归类。Classify the characters according to the number of strokes.

米 来 刀 力 田 手 心 女 子 门 问 想 男 好

2 strokes

3 strokes

4 strokes

5 strokes

6 strokes

7 strokes

13 strokes

4. 将汉字与对应的意思连起来。Match the characters with their meanings.

米	knife
刀	rice
田	field
心	to ask
子	heart
好	son
问	good

来	door
力	hand
手	female
女	to come
门	male
男	to think
想	strength

5. 给下列汉字标注拼音。Write Pinyin for the following characters.

女 手 刀 田 子 男 力

心 来 米 好 门 问 想

课堂活动 Activities

1. 听音抢字卡：老师把汉字卡片悬挂在黑板上，学生分成两组，找出与老师发音相符合的字卡，抢到的字卡多的一组获胜。

   Card picking competition: The class is divided into two groups and compete for picking the character cards on the blackboard which match the teacher's pronunciation. The group with more cards wins.

2. 找朋友：取两套字卡，将学生分成两组，每个学生手头至少分给一张字卡，要求学生迅速举牌拼出已学的合体字，拼对了积一分，拼得越快越好。

   Finding friends: Again the class is divided into two groups and distributed with the following character cards (at least one card per person). The whole class raise cards simultaneously and combine the components on different cards into compound characters. Score one point for one correct combination — the faster, the better.

1）________ 2）________ 3）________ 4）________ 5）________ 6）________

三 语音 | Phonetics

儿化 -r final

"儿 er" 作为后缀时不是单独的音节，而是与它前一音节的韵母结合，形成一个音节，并使这个韵母带上卷舌音色。例如：

The suffix "儿 er" is not a syllable but it's used together with the preceding syllable to make the vowel a retroflex one. For example:

本儿 (běnr notebook)　　门儿 (ménr door)

随堂练 Classroom exercises

听录音并跟读。Read after the recording.

huó — huór	tóu — tóur	bāo — bāor	gài — gàir
tuō — tuōr	diào — diàor	wān — wānr	miàn — miànr
kòng — kòngr	míng — míngr	yǎn — yǎnr	juǎn — juǎnr

语音练习 Phonetic exercises

1. 听录音，在听到的音节下划线。Underline the syllables you hear.

cír	cìr	huàr	huār	nàr	nǎr
yèr	yìnr	dǐr	dìr	xīnr	xìnr
gēr	gèr	jiěr	jiér	gǒur	guǒr
gānr	gāngr	huánr	huángr	xiǎoshìr	xiǎojīr

2. 听写拼音。Pinyin Dictation.

________ ________ ________ ________ ________ ________

________ ________ ________ ________ ________ ________

________ ________ ________ ________ ________ ________

3. 听录音补全句子，然后跟读。Listen to the recording, complete the sentences and read them.

1）Xiànzài ________________. Now we are going to have a dictation.

2）Qǐng ________________, fān dào ________________. Please open your books and turn to Page 1.

3）Qǐng bǎ zuòyè ________________. Please hand in your homework to me.

4）________________ shì shénme? What's the homework for today?

4. 听录音给下列词或短语标注拼音，并猜猜它们的意思。Listen to the recording, write down the Pinyin for the following words and expressions, and guess their meanings.

小刀		不大	
小门		不问	
小口		不来	
小手		不想	
好男好女好心人			
日好月好山水好			
女子好，日月明			

5. 看拼音，读一读下列词语，查查它们的意思。Read the following words by Pinyin and try to find out their meanings in the dictionary.

mǐfàn 米饭	dàmǐ 大米	xiǎomǐ 小米	láihuí 来回	dàdāo 大刀	xiǎodāo 小刀
lìqi 力气	nǔlì 努力	tiándì 田地	nóngtián 农田	shǒubiǎo 手表	shǒujī 手机
xīnqíng 心情	àixīn 爱心	nǚ' ér 女儿	nǚrén 女人	měinǚ 美女	érnǚ 儿女
zǐnǚ 子女	zǐsūn 子孙	érzi 儿子	sūnzi 孙子	ménkǒu 门口	kāimén 开门
guānmén 关门	hǎorén 好人	hǎoshì 好事	měihǎo 美好	nánrén 男人	nánshēng 男生
wèntí 问题	qǐngwèn 请问	xiǎngfǎ 想法	sīxiǎng 思想		

课堂活动 Activities

1. 认读字卡，写出拼音：老师举起本课所学汉字的字卡，要求学生在黑板上写出拼音。

Read character cards and write Pinyin: The teacher raises the character cards of this lesson and asks students to write down the Pinyin on the blackboard.

2. 拼写比赛：老师事先准备好两张写有相同数量拼音的卡片，将学生分为两组，每组由一位同学发音，另一位同学根据其发音在黑板上写出拼音，若写对则可以继续写下一个音，若写错则该组换人。最终使用人数少的一组获胜。

Pinyin competition: The teacher prepares two cards with the same amount of Pinyin and divides the whole class into two groups. One student in each group reads the Pinyin on the card aloud, and another student from the same group transcribes what he/she hears into Pinyin on the blackboard. The one who does correct transcription continues, while the one who makes mistakes should be substituted by another group member. The group with fewer transcribers wins.

四 现学现用 | Survival Chinese

1. 熟读下列句子。Read the following sentences over.

1）Míngbai ma?	Understand?
—— Míngbai le.	— Yes.
—— Bù míngbai.	— No.
2）Wǒmen xiūxi yíxià ba.	Let's have a break.
3）Wǒ jīntiān bù néng qù shàngkè.	I can't go to class today.
4）Duìbuqǐ, wǒ chídào le.	Sorry, I am late.

2. 请将图中人物说的话用汉语再说一遍。Interpret what the people in the pictures say into Chinese.

文化知识 Chinese ABC

汉字的构成（二）
The Formation of Chinese Characters (II)

3 会意字 Associative compounds

Associative compounds combine two or more parts, which individually have an idea, to express a new meaning.

明  "日" (sun) and "月" (moon) are combined to mean "bright".

林  Two "木" (trees) side by side mean "woods" or "forest".

相  A "目" (eye) gazing at a "木" (tree) means "observe".

泪  A "目" (eye) with water means "tear".

4 形声字 Pictophonetic characters

Pictophonetic characters have two elements, one indicating meaning and the other indicating sound. For example, the pronunciation of "问" resembles "门" and the meaning (to ask) is related to "口" (mouth); the pronunciation of "想" resembles "相" and the meaning (to think) is related to "心"(heart).

第六课 Lesson 6 你好！Hello!

语言要点

1 S + adv. + adj.：我很忙。

2 "……吗？"：你忙吗？

3 "……呢？"：我叫马丁。你呢？

一 课文 | Texts

对话一 你好！

[Scene] Martin and Wang Xiaowen meet for the first time. They say hello and get to know each other.

听录音并朗读
Listen to the recording and read aloud

Wáng Xiǎowén: Nǐ hǎo!
王小文：你好！

Mǎ Dīng: Nǐ hǎo!
马丁：你好！

Wáng Xiǎowén: Qǐngwèn, nǐ jiào shénme míngzi?
王小文：请问，你叫什么名字？①

Mǎ Dīng: Wǒ jiào Mǎ Dīng. Nǐ ne?
马丁：我叫马丁。你呢？

Wáng Xiǎowén: Wǒ jiào Wáng Xiǎowén.
王小文：我叫王小文。

Notes

① 你叫什么名字？What's your name?
"你叫什么名字？"只用于问同辈或年龄较小的人的姓名。
"你叫什么名字？" applies only to one's peers and the younger.

你	nǐ	*pron.*	you (singular)
你好	nǐ hǎo		hello
请	qǐng	*v.*	please
请问	qǐngwèn	*v.*	excuse me (before a question)
叫	jiào	*v.*	to be named; to be called
什么	shénme	*pron.*	what
名字	míngzi	*n.*	name
我	wǒ	*pron.*	I; me
呢	ne	*particle*	(used at the end of an interrogative sentence)

对话二　你忙吗？

[Scene] Daming and his old friend Martin say greetings when they come across each other.

听录音并朗读
Listen to the recording and read aloud

Dàmíng: Nǐ máng ma?
大明：你 忙 吗？

Mǎ Dīng: Hěn máng. Nǐ ne?
马 丁：很 忙。你 呢？

Dàmíng: Wǒ bù máng.
大明：我不 忙。

Mǎ Dīng: Nǐ bàba、 māma hǎo ma?
马 丁：你 爸爸、妈妈 好 吗？

Dàmíng: Tāmen hěn hǎo.
大明：他们 很 好。

忙	máng	*adj.*	busy
吗	ma	*particle*	(used at the end of a statement to transform it into a question)
很	hěn	*adv.*	very
不	bù	*adv.*	not; no
爸爸	bàba	*n.*	dad
妈妈	māma	*n.*	mum
他们	tāmen	*pron.*	they; them
们	men	*suffix*	(plural marker for pronouns and a few animate nouns)

短文 她很忙

听录音、朗读并且复述
Listen to the recording, read aloud, and then retell

Tā jiào Wáng Xiǎowén.
她叫王小文。

Tā hěn máng.
她很忙。

Nǐ ne? Nǐ jiào shénme míngzi?
你呢？你叫什么名字？

Nǐ máng ma?
你忙吗？

她	tā	*pron.*	she; her

二 语言要点 Key points

1 我很忙。

先看句子：Read the examples first:

1）我很忙。 I am busy. 我不忙。 I am not busy.

2）他们 很 好。 They are well. 他们 不 好。 They are not well.

S + adv. + adj.

汉语中形容词可以做谓语，但形容词前面一般要加上“很”、“不”、“非常”、“有点儿”等副词。

In the Chinese language, an adjective can function as the predicate of a sentence, but usually with adverbs in front, such as “很”, “不”, “非常 (very)”, “有点儿 (a little)”, etc.

提示 Be aware

表示两者比较时，形容词前可以不加副词。例如：

When expressing comparison, there could be no adverbs before the adjective. For example:

他忙，我不忙。

汉&英 Chinese vs. English

英语句子中的形容词前往往有"to be"，汉语中没有这一成分。例如：

In an English sentence, "to be" is usually before the adjective. This is not the case in Chinese. For example:

1）我很好。　I am fine.

2）她不忙。　She is not busy.

2 你忙吗？

先看句子：Read the examples first:

1）A: 你忙吗？　Are you busy?

　 B: 我不忙。　I am not busy.

2）A: 你爸爸、妈妈好吗？　Are your parents fine?

　 B: 他们很好。　They are fine.

"……吗？"是是非疑问句的一种。

"……吗？" is one way of asking a "yes/no" question.

汉&英 Chinese vs. English

- 跟英语的是非疑问句不同的是，汉语中回答问题只需直接陈述答案，无需先说"是，……"或"不，……"。例如：

  Different from the answer to an English "yes/no" question, the reply in Chinese is a direct statement instead of "yes" or "no" first. For example:

  A: 你忙吗？　Are you busy?

  B: 我很忙。/　Yes, I am busy./

  　 我不忙。　No, I am not busy.

- 在回答用"……吗？"提出的问题时，可以简略回答。例如：

  The answers to questions like "……吗？" could be in the shortened form. For example:

  A: 你忙吗？　Are you busy?

  B: 很忙。/ 忙。　Yes, I am very busy./ Yes, I am busy.

3 我叫马丁。你呢？

先看句子：Read the examples first:

1）我叫小文。	My name is Xiaowen.
你呢？（你叫什么名字？）	How about you? (What's your name?)
2）A：你忙吗？	Are you busy?
B：我不忙。	I am not busy.
你呢？（你忙吗？）	How about you? (Are you busy?)

对话中，在语境明确的情况下，可以用"……呢？"提问，以避免重复。

In a conversation, if the context is clear, the question could be "……呢？" to avoid repetition.

三 语音 | Phonetics

"不"的变调 The Sandhi of "不"

"不"，原调为"bù"。"不"在第一、第二、第三声字前读原调"bù"，在第四声字前变为"bú"。

The original pronunciation of "不" is "bù". When it is before a character of the first, second or third tone, "不" is read as "bù". When it is before a character of the fourth tone, "不" is pronounced as "bú".

不多 (多 many; much)	不忙	不好	不大
bù duō	bù máng	bù hǎo	bú dà

随堂练 Classroom exercises

听录音并跟读。Read after the recording.

"不"＋第一声（1st tone）：	bù tīng	bù shuō	bù kū	bù xiān	bù gāo
"不"＋第二声（2nd tone）：	bù xíng	bù cháng	bù lái	bù nán	bù hóng
"不"＋第三声（3rd tone）：	bù xiǎng	bù měi	bù zǒu	bù shǎo	bù xiǎo
"不"＋第四声（4th tone）：	bú qù	bú shì	bú zuò	bú duì	bú huì

四　练习 | Exercises

1. 给“不”标上实际的声调。Mark the tone of “不” in spoken Chinese.

bu xīn	bu xiāng	bu chī	bu zhī
bu hán	bu néng	bu zhí	bu rú
bu dǒng	bu lǐ	bu zhǐ	bu gěi
bu guì	bu zài	bu xìn	bu lèi

2. 听老师的发音，给下列词语标注声调并跟读，注意两组词意义的区别。Listen to the teacher's pronunciation, mark the tones and read after the teacher. Pay attention to the difference between the two groups.

dongxi	east and west	dongxi	things
maimai	business	maimai	buy and sell
duitou	enemy; rival	duitou	correct
didao	tunnel	didao	pure; typical

3. 听录音，给下列词语标上声调，然后大声朗读，试试在后续的练习中运用这些词汇。Listen to the recording, mark the tones and read aloud. Try to use these words in the following exercises.

Singular		Plural		Possessive case		Honorific form
你ni	you	你们nimen	you	你的nide	your	您 nin you
我wo	I; me	我们women	we	我的wode	my	
他ta	he; him	他们tamen	them	他的tade	his	
她ta	she; her	她们tamen	them	她的tade	her	
它ta	it	它们tamen	them	它的tade	its	

4. 教师准备好生词卡片，让学生读出其所抽取的词语，并标注拼音。Students pick out one vocabulary card from those presented by the teacher, read it aloud and write down the Pinyin.

名字　什么　爸爸　我们　妈妈

叫　忙　好　很　呢　你

5. 选择填空。Fill in the blanks.

吗　呢

1）你爸爸、妈妈好________？
2）我爸爸、妈妈很好。你爸爸、妈妈________？
3）他们忙________？
4）我不忙，你________？

6. 完成下列对话。Complete the following conversations.

1）A：你忙__________？
B：__________。
A：你爸爸、妈妈__________？
B：他们__________。

2）A：你叫__________？
B：我叫马丁。你__________？
A：我叫小文。你忙吗？
B：__________。你呢？
A：__________。

7. 根据课文内容回答问题。Answer the questions according to the texts.

1）马丁忙吗？大明呢？
2）大明的爸爸、妈妈好吗？
3）短文中的“她”叫什么名字？“她”忙吗？

8. 翻译下列句子。Translation.

1）I am fine.
2）I am not busy.

3）My name is Daming.

4）What's your name?

课堂活动 Activities

1. 学生两人一组，根据自己的情况，完成下列对话。

   Make dialogues in pairs according to the real situation.

   A：你叫什么名字？
   B：我叫__________。你__________？
   A：我叫__________。你忙吗？
   B：__________。你呢？
   A：我__________。

2. 全班学生按照下面的句子，循环进行自我介绍和交换介绍。

   Everyone introduces oneself and others in the following pattern in class.

   我叫__________。
   我__________忙。
   他/她叫__________。
   他/她__________忙。

五 字、词、句 | Character, word, and sentence

1. 认读

读一读，猜一猜。Read and guess.

我	I; me	我们 / 我的 / 我很忙。/ 我叫大山。
们	*suffix (for pl.)*	你们 / 我们 / 他们 / 她们 / 人们
名	name	名字 / 大名 / 小名 / 人名 / 地名 (dìmíng)

字	character	文字 / 汉字 (Hànzì)
忙	busy	很忙 / 不忙 / 忙吗？
不	not	不好 / 不忙 / 不大 / 不是 (bùshì) / 不来 / 不问 / 不想
很	very	很好 / 很忙 / 很大 / 很小 / 很少
吗	*particle*	好吗？ / 大吗？ / 你忙吗？ / 他来吗？
你	you	你们 / 你好 / 你呢？ / 你忙吗？ / 你叫什么名字？

2. 音义

1）将汉字与其相对应的读音和意思连起来。Match the characters with their Pinyin and meanings.

nǐ	字	very
bù	你	character
máng	不	busy
hěn	忙	not
zì	很	you

2）填空。Fill in the blanks.

① 你叫什么__________字？

② 他们好__________？

③ 我__________忙，__________呢？

④ 她爸爸、妈妈__________好。

3）用下列汉字组词，比一比，看谁组的词语多。Make words with the following characters — the more, the better.

不：

们：

忙：

我：

很：

字：

名：

3. 书写

写汉字，注意笔画笔顺。Write the following Chinese characters and pay attention to the stroke order.

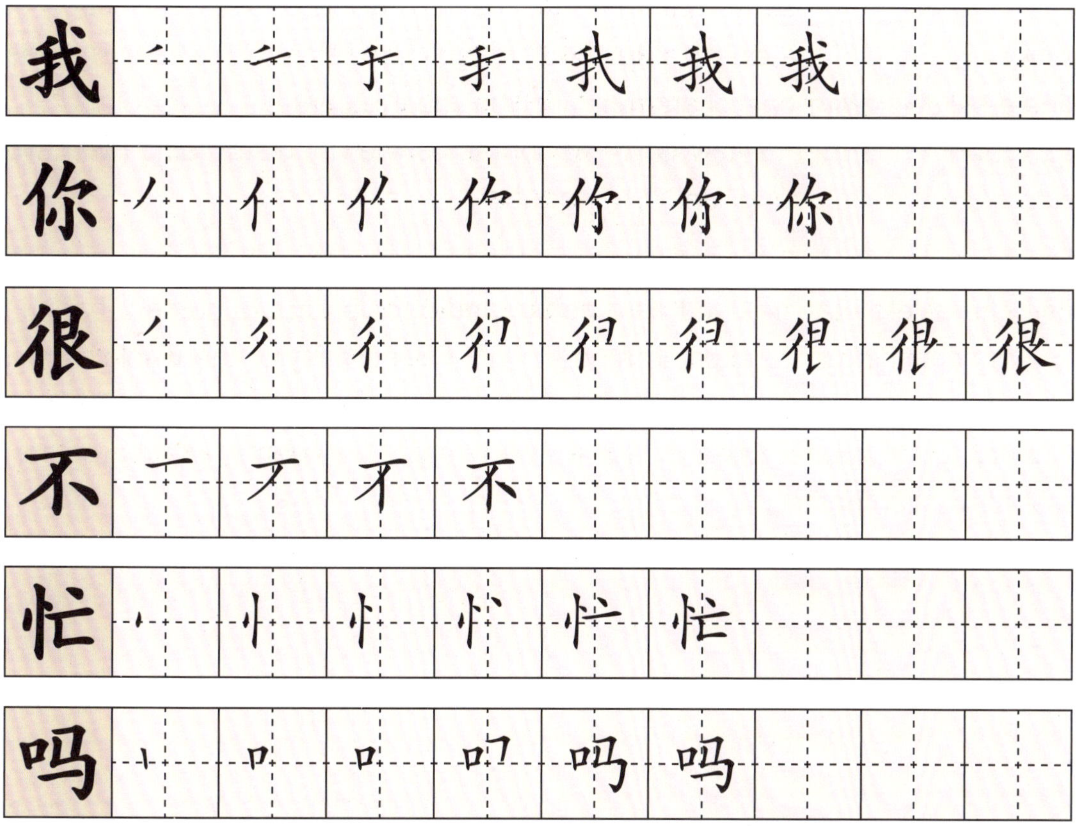

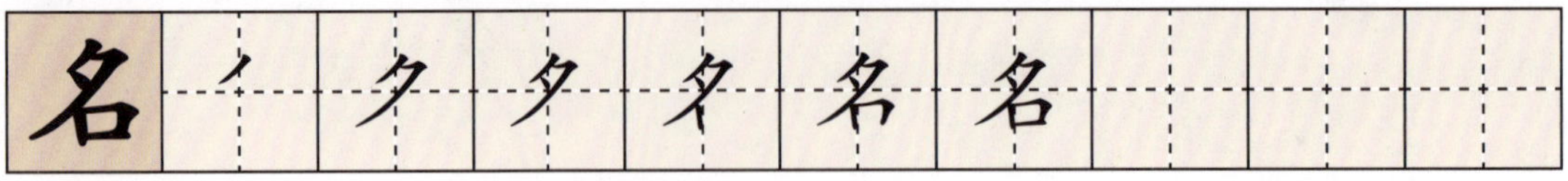

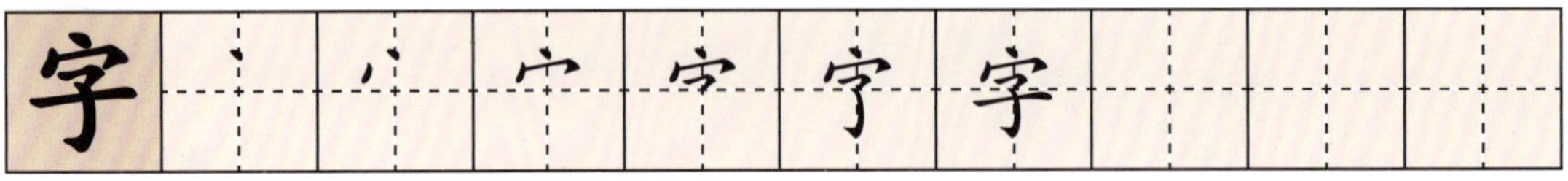

文化知识
Chinese ABC

中国人的姓名
Chinese Names

A Chinese name is composed of two parts: the surname and the given name. The surname goes before the given name. For instance, in the name "Lǐ Míng", "Lǐ", as the surname, goes before the given name "Míng".

The common Chinese surnames are collected in the book *A Collection of Surnames* (《百家姓》), a classical textbook for children. Most Chinese surnames are single-syllabic (with one character) like the most commonly used ones "Lǐ", "Wáng", "Zhāng" and "Liú". A few Chinese surnames are double-syllabic (with two characters) such as "Ōuyáng" and "Shàngguān".

There are no "regular names" (like the Christian names) in Chinese. In fact, all Chinese characters may be used as a name, and people tend to name a baby in memory of something or to express a good wish for the baby or the whole family. The given name can have either one character or two. For example, in "Lǐ Míng", "Míng" is the given name; while in "Wáng Xiǎowén", "Xiǎowén" (two characters) serves as the given name.

第七课 Lesson 7

我介绍一下

Allow me to introduce you to each other

语言要点

1 ……是……：我是美国人。

2 pron./n. + 的 + n.：我的朋友

3 “也”的用法：他也学习汉语。

一 课文 | Texts

对话一 您贵姓？

[Scene] In his first class, Martin meets his teacher, Mr. Lin.

听录音并朗读
Listen to the recording and read aloud

Mǎ Dīng: Lǎoshī, qǐngwèn nín guìxìng?
马丁：老师，请问您贵姓？①

Lín lǎoshī: Wǒ xìng Lín.
林老师：我姓林。

Mǎ Dīng: Lín lǎoshī, nín hǎo!
马丁：林老师②，您好！

Lín lǎoshī: Nǐ hǎo! Nǐ jiào shénme míngzi?
林老师：你好！你叫什么名字？

Mǎ Dīng: Wǒ jiào Mǎ Dīng.
马丁：我叫马丁。

Lín lǎoshī: Nǐ shì nǎ guó rén?
林老师：你是哪国人？③

Mǎ Dīng: Wǒ shì Měiguórén.
马丁：我是美国人。

Notes

① 您贵姓？May I ask your surname?
这是询问他人姓氏比较礼貌的表达法。
It's a polite expression when asking about the surname of the other side of the conversation.

② 林老师 Mr. Lin
中国人称呼他人时，将姓放在称谓的前边，如：王老师、林大夫。
In addressing other people, the Chinese custom is to place the surname before the title. For example, "Wáng lǎoshī" and "Lín dàifu".

③ 你是哪国人？Which country are you from?
用于询问对方的国籍。
This sentence is used to ask about the nationality.

老师	lǎoshī	*n.*	teacher
您	nín	*pron.*	you (polite form)
贵姓	guìxìng	*n.*	surname (polite form)
姓	xìng	*v.*	one's surname is...
		n.	surname
是	shì	*v.*	to be (am/is/are)
哪	nǎ	*pron.*	which
国	guó	*n.*	country
美国	Měiguó	*n.*	the U.S.A.

对话二　我介绍一下

[Scene] Martin and Daming meet Mr. Lin in the campus. Martin introduces Daming to Mr. Lin.

听录音并朗读

Listen to the recording and read aloud

Mǎ Dīng: Lín lǎoshī, nín hǎo! Wǒ jièshào yíxià,
马丁：林老师，您好！我介绍一下，①

zhè shì wǒ de péngyou Dàmíng.
这是我的朋友大明。②

Lín lǎoshī: Nǐ hǎo!
林老师：（对大明）你好！

Dàmíng: Lín lǎoshī hǎo!
大明：林老师好！

Lín lǎoshī: Nǐ yě xué Hànyǔ ma?
林老师：你也学汉语吗？

Dàmíng: Duì, wǒ yě xué Hànyǔ.
大明：对，我也学汉语。

Lín lǎoshī: Nǐ yě shì Měiguórén ma?
林老师：你也是美国人吗？

Dàmíng: Wǒ bú shì Měiguórén, wǒ shì Yīngguórén.
大明：我不是美国人，我是英国人。

Notes

① 我介绍一下。Let me introduce you to each other.

“一下”一般用在动词后，表示动作时间短、尝试或轻松的意味。

“一下” is generally used after a verb, indicating its shortness, tentativeness, and leisureliness.

② 这是我的朋友。This is my friend.

在介绍时，常常用“是”引出人的名字、身份、国籍等内容。在介绍别人时，通常说“这是……”，比较礼貌。

During an introduction, the person's name, identity and nationality are usually led by “是”. The polite form “这是……” is often used when introducing others.

介绍	jièshào	*v.*	to introduce
一	yī	*num.*	one
一下	yīxià	*adv.*	(used after a verb as its complement, indicating a brief action or an attempt)
这	zhè	*pron.*	this
的	de	*particle*	(used after an attribute to indicate a modifying and modified relationship)
朋友	péngyou	*n.*	friend
也	yě	*adv.*	too; also
学	xué	*v.*	to study; to learn
汉语	Hànyǔ	*n.*	Chinese language
对	duì	*adj.*	right; correct
英国	Yīngguó	*n.*	the U.K.

短文 他也学习汉语

听录音、朗读并且复述
Listen to the recording, read aloud, and then retell

Dàjiā hǎo! Wǒ jièshào yíxià, wǒ jiào Mǎ Dīng. Wǒ shì Měiguórén, wǒ shì xuésheng, wǒ xué Hànyǔ. Zhè shì wǒ de péngyou, tā jiào Dàmíng. Tā shì Yīngguórén, tā yě xué Hànyǔ.

大家好！我介绍一下，我叫马丁。我是美国人，我是学生，我学汉语。这是我的朋友，他叫大明。他是英国人，他也学汉语。

大家	dàjiā	*pron.*	everyone
学生	xuésheng	*n.*	student

二 语言要点 | Key points

1 我是美国人。

先看句子：Read the examples first:

1）我是大明。 I am Daming.

2）她是美国人。 She is an American.

3）这是林老师。 This is Mr. Lin.

4）我是学生，他是老师。 I am a student. He is a teacher.

5）他不是美国人。 He is not an American.

"是"意思是"to be (am/is/are)"。否定形式是"……不是……"。

"是" means "to be (am/is/are)". Its negative form is "……不是……".

2 我的朋友

先看短语：Read the examples first:

1）他的朋友 his friend

2）我的老师 my teacher

3）大明的爸爸 Daming's father

4）我的书 my book

"的"可以表示领属关系。

Here "的" indicates possession.

▶ 提示 Be aware

在表示家人、亲属等紧密关系时，人称代词"我"、"你"、"他"和"她"后可以不用"的"，其他情况下一般保留"的"。例如：

When indicating close relationship such as family membership or kinship, the "的" after a personal pronoun, such as "我", "你", "他" or "她", is optional, while in other circumstances the "的" is compulsory. For examlpe:

1）我的妈妈 / 我妈妈 my mother

2）她的妹妹 / 她妹妹 her sister

3）王老师的爸爸 Mr. Wang's father

3 他也学习汉语。

先看句子：Read the examples first:

1）我学习汉语，他也学习汉语。 I study Chinese, and he also studies Chinese.

2）马丁是学生，大明也是学生。 Martin is a student, and Daming is also a student.

3）爸爸很忙，妈妈也很忙。 Dad is busy, and mum is also busy.

"也" 表示所说的事物与前面的事物有相同之处。

"也" indicates that the subject shares something in common with the former one.

提示 Be aware

汉语中的"也"放在动词或形容词前，不能放在主语前，也不能放在句末。下面这些句子都是错的：

In a Chinese sentence, "也" goes immediately before the verb or the adjective, but never before the subject or at the end of the sentence. The sentences below are all wrong:

1）我学习汉语，也他学习汉语。（×）

2）马丁是学生，大明是也学生。（×）

3）爸爸很忙，妈妈很忙也。（×）

三 语音 | Phonetics

"一"的变调 The sandhi of "一"

我们学过的"一"，只有在表示个位数目、序数以及处于词语末尾时才读原调yī。例如：

"一" pronounces as "yī" only when it indicates number counting, ordinal numbers, or is at the end of a word or expression. For example:

yī（一）	shíyī（十一）
dì-yī（第一）	chūyī（初一）

其他情况下的实际发音请看下表：

Other cases are shown in the following form:

一天	一年 (year)	一点儿	一次 (time)
yì tiān	yì nián	yìdiǎnr	yí cì

“一”在第一、第二、第三声字前读“yì”，在第四声字前读“yí”。

The pronunciation of “一” before a character of the first, second or third tone is “ yì ”; while the pronunciation of “一” before a character of the fourth tone is “ yí ”.

随 堂 练
Classroom exercises

听录音并跟读。Read after the recording.

“一” + 第一声（1st tone）：	yì jiān	yì fēng	yì kē	yì jīn
“一” + 第二声（2nd tone）：	yì pán	yì tuán	yì tiáo	yì huí
“一” + 第三声（3rd tone）：	yì zhǒng	yì tǒng	yì juǎn	yì bǎ
“一” + 第四声（4th tone）：	yí gè	yí piàn	yí jiàn	yí wèi

四 练习 | Exercises

1. 给“一”标上实际的声调。Mark the tone of “一” in spoken Chinese.

yi piān	yi shuāng	yixiē	yi fēn
yi rén	yi qún	yi yuán	yi máo
yi kǒu	yidiǎn	yiqǐ	yi pǐ
yigòng	yi biàn	yi kuài	yixià

2. 听录音，在你听到的拼音后打“√”。Listen and mark the one you hear with a “√” after it.

yǎnsè ○	yánsè ○	zhùzi ○	zhúzi ○	xiězuò ○	xiézuò ○
tōngzhī ○	tóngzhì ○	jiǎnhuà ○	jiǎnghuà ○	liànxí ○	liánxì ○
qièshí ○	quèshí ○	tiān lán ○	tiānrán ○		

3. 听录音，给下列词语标上声调，然后大声朗读，试试在后续的练习中运用这些词汇。Listen to the recording, mark the tones and read aloud. Try to use these words in the following exercises.

Yingguo 英国	Faguo 法国	Deguo 德国	Xibanya 西班牙	Hanguo 韩国	Riben 日本
Yingyu 英语	Fayu 法语	Deyu 德语	Xibanyayu 西班牙语	Hanyu 韩语	Riyu 日语

4. 朗读下列句子并标注拼音。Read the following sentences and write down their Pinyin.

1）我介绍一下。 ______________________

2）他不是学生。 ______________________

3）我也学习汉语。 ______________________

4）他是我的朋友。 ______________________

5）你是英国人吗？ ______________________

5. 选择填空。Fill in the blanks.

1）他们学习不________忙。

2）我爸爸、妈妈________很好。

3）我________美国人。

4）她不________学生。

是

×

1）我________一下儿，这位________林老师。
2）他________大明，是我________朋友。
3）我学习汉语，他________学习汉语。
4）他________是美国人，是英国人。

是	叫	介绍
的	也	不

6. 组词成句。Make sentences with the randomly placed words in each group.

1）忙　也　我们　很
2）吗　也　你　学生　是
3）也　他们　我的朋友　是
4）不　美国人　我们　是

7. 完成下列对话。Complete the following conversations.

1）A：________________？
B：我姓田，你叫我田老师吧。

2）A：________________？
B：我叫马丁。
A：________________？
B：我是美国人。
A：________________？
B：我是学生，________________？
A：我也是学生。

3）A：我介绍一下，________________。
B：林老师，您好！
林老师：你好！________________？
B：对，我也学汉语。

8. 模仿课文中的短文写一个简短的自我介绍，也可介绍一下自己的朋友。Write a passage to introduce yourself or one of your friends in the form of the passage of this lesson.

课堂活动
Activities

1. 根据课文介绍一下马丁和大明。
   Introduce Martin and Daming according to the texts.

2. 三人一组，轮流询问姓名和国籍。
   Form a group of three and ask about each other's name and nationality in turn.

3. 三人一组，轮流由其中一人为另外两人作介绍。
   Form a group of three and introduce the other two group members in turn.

五 字、词、句 | Character, word, and sentence

1. 认读

读一读，猜一猜。Read and guess.

他	he; him	他们 / 他的 / 他叫大明。/ 他是学生。/ 他学习（xuéxí）汉语。
老	*prefix* old	老师 老人 / 老家（lǎojiā）/ 老朋友 / 老白 / 老林
国	country; state	中国（Zhōngguó）/ 美国 / 英国 / 国家 / 国力 / 大国 / 小国
是	to be	不是 / 他是美国人。/ 我不是老师。/ 这是你妈妈吗？
学	to study	学生 / 同学（tóngxué）/ 学习 / 大学 / 中学 / 小学 / 学什么 / 学中文 / 学汉语 / 文学
生	student	学生 / 女生 / 男生 / 师生 / 新生（xīnshēng）
姓	one's surname is...; surname	姓名 / 您贵姓？/ 他姓什么？/ 我姓林。
语	language	语言（yǔyán）/ 口语 / 汉语 / 日语 / 英语 / 法语（fǎyǔ）/ 语法

2. 音义

1）教师准备好生词卡片，让学生读出其所抽取的词语，并标注拼音。Students pick out a word card from those presented by the teacher, read it aloud and write down the Pinyin.

国家　语言　同学　师生　老人　不是　他们　贵姓

2）用下列汉字组词，比一比，看谁组的词语多。Make words with the following characters — the more, the better.

生：

学：

国：

语：

3）写出下列词语的拼音和意思。Write down the Pinyin and meanings of the following words.

口语____________、____________　老家____________、____________

新生____________、____________　姓名____________、____________

小学____________、____________　老朋友__________、____________

3. 书写

写汉字，注意笔画笔顺。Write the following Chinese characters and pay attention to the stroke order.

文化知识
Chinese ABC

中国人的称谓

Addressing People in Chinese

The common practice is to address people with both the surname and the given name. A double-syllabic given name without a surname before sounds close and thus can be used on an informal occasion. For instance, Wang Xiaowen's parents might call her "Xiǎowén" at home. A single-syllabic given name is not usually used independently unless between couples. Sometimes people tend to alter it to a double-syllabic name, like "Lǐ Míng" could be called "Míngming" or "Xiǎomíng" by his relatives or friends.

To address others in the Chinese society, it is polite to use the surname before a title. The full name or given name is used only by one's relatives and friends. At work places, it is appropriate to address a person by his rank or profession, and on the social occasions, you can make it more flexible. When you demand a stranger's name, you can say "Zěnme chēnghū nín?" If it is an elderly person or your senior, "Nǐ jiào shénme míngzi?" may sound rude. Instead, "Nín guìxìng?" is socially acceptable.

When you have known the person's surname, you can use it before his title, such as "Lǐ lǎoshī (teacher)", "Zhāng jīnglǐ (manager)", "Liú shīfu (master)" etc.

第八课 Lesson 8
她是谁？ Who is she?

语言要点

1 用“谁”提问：她是谁？

2 ……有/没有……：我有哥哥，没有姐姐。

3 A 和 B：我爸爸、妈妈、弟弟和妹妹在美国。

一 课文 | Texts

对话一 她是谁?

[Scene] Wang Xiaowen sees a photo of Martin's family. Martin introduces his family members to her.

听录音并朗读
Listen to the recording and read aloud

Wáng Xiǎowén: Zhè shì nǐmen jiā de zhàopiàn ma?
王 小文：这 是 你们 家 的 照片 吗？

Mǎ Dīng: Duì. Zhè shì wǒ bàba, zhè shì wǒ māma,
马 丁：对。这 是 我 爸爸，这 是 我 妈妈，

zhè shì wǒ mèimei, nà shì wǒ dìdi.
这 是 我 妹妹，那 是 我 弟弟。

Wáng Xiǎowén: Tā shì shéi?
王 小文：她 是 谁？

Mǎ Dīng: Tā shì wǒ de nǚpéngyou.
马 丁：她 是 我 的 女朋友。

Wáng Xiǎowén: Tā hěn piàoliang! Tā shì nǎ guó rén?
王 小文：她 很 漂亮！她 是 哪 国 人？

Mǎ dīng: Tā yě shì Měiguórén.
马 丁：她 也 是 美国人。

你们	nǐmen	*pron.*	you (plural form)
家	jiā	*n.*	home; family
照片	zhàopiàn	*n.*	photo
妹妹	mèimei	*n.*	younger sister
那	nà	*pron.*	that
弟弟	dìdi	*n.*	younger brother
谁	shéi	*pron.*	who; whom
女朋友	nǚpéngyou	*n.*	girlfriend
漂亮	piàoliang	*adj.*	pretty; beautiful

对话二　你有哥哥、姐姐吗？

[Scene] Martin is introducing his family members.

听录音并朗读
Listen to the recording and read aloud

Wáng Xiǎowén: Mǎ Dīng, nǐ yǒu gēge、 jiějie ma?
王小文：马丁，你有哥哥、姐姐吗？

Mǎ Dīng: Wǒ yǒu gēge, méiyǒu jiějie, nǐ ne?
马丁：我有哥哥，没有姐姐，你呢？

Wáng Xiǎowén: Wǒ méiyǒu gēge, yě méiyǒu jiějie.
王小文：我没有哥哥，也没有姐姐。

Mǎ Dīng: Wǒ bàba、māma、dìdi hé mèimei zài
马丁：我爸爸、妈妈、弟弟和妹妹在

Měiguó, wǒ gēge zài Rìběn, tā xué Rìyǔ.
美国，我哥哥在日本，他学日语。

有	yǒu	*v.*	to have
哥哥	gēge	*n.*	elder brother
姐姐	jiějie	*n.*	elder sister
没	méi	*v.*	not
没有	méiyǒu	*v.*	have not
和	hé	*conj.*	and
在	zài	*v.*	be in/at/on
日本	Rìběn	*n.*	Japan
日语	Rìyǔ	*n.*	Japanese (language)

短文 现在我在中国

听录音、朗读并且复述

Listen to the recording, read aloud, and then retell

Dàjiā hǎo, wǒ jiào Mǎ Dīng, wǒ shì Měiguórén.
大家好，我叫马丁，我是美国人。

Xiànzài wǒ zài Zhōngguó. Wǒ xué Hànyǔ.
现在我在中国。我学汉语。

Wǒ de nǚpéngyou yě shì Měiguórén, tā hěn piàoliang, tā yě
我的女朋友也是美国人，她很漂亮，她也

xué Hànyǔ. Wǒ de bàba、māma、dìdi hé mèimei zài Měiguó,
学汉语。我的爸爸、妈妈、弟弟和妹妹在美国，

wǒ gēge zài Rìběn, tā xué Rìyǔ.
我哥哥在日本，他学日语。

现在	xiànzài	*n.*	now

二 语言要点 | Key points

1 她是谁?

先看句子：Read the examples first:

1）A: 她是谁? Who is she?

B: 她是我的女朋友。 She is my girlfriend.

2）A: 谁是你的老师? Who is your teacher?

B: 他是我的老师。 He is my teacher.

3）A: 他是谁的老师? Whose teacher is he?

B: 他是我的老师。 He is my teacher.

在汉语中，特殊疑问句的语序和陈述句的语序一致，只需把未知信息换成疑问代词。

In Chinese, the word order of a special question (Wh-question) is the same as that of a declarative sentence, just to replace the unknown information with a question word.

2 我有哥哥，没有姐姐。

"S + 有 + O" 意思是 "sb. has sth."，句型见下表：

"S + 有 + O" means "sb. has sth." Here are the sentence patterns:

Positive sentence	Negative sentence	"Yes/No" question
S + 有 + O	**S + 没（有）+ O**	**S + 有 + O + 吗?**
我有哥哥。	我没（有）姐姐。	你有哥哥吗?
I have an elder brother.	I have no elder sisters.	Do you have elder brothers?

提示 Be aware

通常，"S + v." 或 "S + adj." 句子的否定形式是 "S + 不 + v./adj."，而 "有" 的否定句是 "S + 没(有) + O"。试比较：

Usually, the negative form of "S + v."or "S + adj." sentences is "S + 不 + v./adj.", but the negative form of "有" sentence is "S + 没(有) + O". Compare the following sentences:

S + V + O	positive sentence	我是美国人。	I am American.
S + 不 + V + O	negative sentence	我不是美国人。	I am not American.
S + 很 + adj.	positive sentence	我很忙。	I am busy.
S + 不 + adj.	negative sentence	我不忙。	I am not busy.
S + 有 + O	positive sentence	我有哥哥。	I have an elder brother.
S + 没(有) + O	negative sentence	我没（有）姐姐。	I have no elder sisters.

3 我爸爸、妈妈、弟弟和妹妹在美国。

先看句子：Read the examples first:

1）我的弟弟和妹妹在美国。My younger brother and younger sister are in the U.S.A.

2）大明和马丁是我的朋友。Daming and Martin are my friends.

“和”用于连接名词或名词短语，表示并列关系。

“和” is used to connect nouns or noun phrases to indicate the parallel relationship.

提示 Be aware

- 连接多个名词时，“和”通常在最后一个名词前，如：
  When connecting several nouns, “和” usually goes before the last noun. For example:
  我的爸爸、妈妈、哥哥和弟弟在美国。
  My father, mother, elder brother and younger brother are in the U.S.A.

- “和”不能用于连接两个形容词或者两个句子，如：
  In Chinese, “和” cannot be used for the conjunction of two adjectives or sentences. For example:
  1）他忙和累（lèi tired）。（×）
  2）我是学生，和我学习汉语。（×）

三 练习 | Exercises

1. 左手还是右手：听老师的发音，如果是A音请举左手，如果是B音请举右手。做完后再读一读A、B两组，注意二者的区别。Left hand or right hand: Listen to the teacher and raise your hand accordingly — left hand for Column A and right hand for Column B. Then read the two columns and pay attention to their differences.

A	B
jiě	qiě
jiā	qiā
zuò	cuò
zū	cū
zhān	chān
zhōu	chōu
diǎn	jiǎn
tàng	dàng
tiāo	diāo
kē	gē
piān	biān

A	B
wǔtiān	wǔdiǎn
zìdiǎn	cídiǎn
cǎisè	cāicè
qíjì	jíqí
jìzhě	qíchē
zàijiàn	cǎidiàn
gèrén	kèrén
zhīdào	chídào
zuìhòu	suíhòu
chángcháng	chángzhǎng
bǎole	pǎole

2. 听录音，说出音节的韵母是左边的还是右边的。Listen to the recording, and tell the finals are on the left or on the right side.

ia	ua
ie	uo
iao	uai
iou	uei

3. 听老师的发音，给下列词语标注声调并跟读。Listen to the teacher's pronunciation, mark the tones and read after the teacher.

baba	didi	jiujiu	meimei
mama	gugu	shushu	gege
yeye	jiejie	nainai	gonggong
ayi	waigong	waipo	popo

4. 听录音，给下列词语标上声调，然后大声朗读，试试在后续的练习中运用这些词汇。Listen to the recording, mark the tones and read aloud. Try to use these words in the following exercises.

Father's side			Mother's side		
爷爷	yeye	grandfather	外公	waigong	grandfather
奶奶	nainai	grandmother	外婆	waipo	grandmother
叔叔	shushu	uncle (father's younger brother)	舅舅	jiujiu	uncle (mother's brother)
姑姑	gugu	aunt (father's sister)	阿姨	ayi	aunt (mother's sister)

5. 选择填空。Fill in the blanks.

1）我________有哥哥，也________有姐姐。
2）他________忙。
3）这________是我们家的照片。
4）我________有女朋友。
5）我的日语________好。

没　不

1）我的妈妈________美国。
2）________是你的女朋友？
3）你的女朋友是________国人？
4）A：你是学生吗？
　　B：________，我是学生。
5）A：你________女朋友吗？
　　B：我________没有女朋友。
6）我的姐姐________妹妹在日本。

哪　谁　对　有　和　在　现在

6. 根据课文完成下面的对话。Complete the conversations according to the texts.

1）王小文：这是你们________的________吗？
　　马丁：对。这是我爸爸，这是我妈妈，这是我________，那是我________。
　　王小文：她是________？
　　马丁：她是我的________。
　　王小文：她很漂亮！她是________人？
　　马丁：她也是美国人。

2）王小文：马丁，你________哥哥、姐姐吗？
　　马丁：我________哥哥，________姐姐，你呢？
　王小文：我没有哥哥，也没有姐姐。
　　马丁：我爸爸、妈妈、弟弟________妹妹________美国，我哥哥在________，他学________。

7. 根据课文内容回答问题。Answer the questions according to the texts.

1）马丁有女朋友吗？
2）马丁的女朋友是哪国人？
3）王小文有没有哥哥、姐姐？
4）马丁的哥哥现在在美国吗？
5）马丁的哥哥学习中文吗？

8. 翻译下列句子。Translation.

1）Do you have a girlfriend?
2）Do you have an elder brother?
3）Your girlfriend is very pretty.
4）Who is your teacher?
5）Now I study Chinese in China.
6）I study Japanese and Chinese.

课堂活动 Activities

1. 每个人用"……有……"向老师或其他同学提一个问题，并回答对方的提问。
Everyone asks a question with "……有……" to the teacher or classmates and answers others' questions.

2. 完成下面的短文。
Complete the passage.

大家好，我叫______，我是______国人。现在我在______，我学习______。我有哥哥，没有姐姐，我们家有六口①人：爸爸、妈妈、哥哥、弟弟、妹妹和我。这是我的______，他/她在______。那是我的______，他/她在______。

[Note]① "口" is a measure word here and it's only used for counting family members.

3. 请带一张自己全家的照片，用本课学习的内容，介绍一下自己的家庭成员。

Bring a family photo and introduce your family members to the class with what you have learned in this lesson.

四 字、词、句 | Character, word, and sentence

1. 认读

读一读，猜一猜。Read and guess.

有	to have	没有 / 有女朋友 / 有哥哥 / 没有哥哥 / 有名
在	be in/at/on	在家 / 不在 / 在中国 / 在北京（Běijīng）/ 在山上 / 他在吗？
和	and	我和你 / 爸爸和妈妈 / 老师和学生 / 中国和美国 / 汉语和日语
女	female	女人 / 女老师 / 女学生 / 女朋友 / 女孩儿（nǚháir）
男	male	男人 / 男老师 / 男学生 / 男朋友 / 男孩儿
谁	who; whom	谁的老师 / 谁的女朋友 / 谁的书（shū）/ 谁的学生 / 你找谁？
人	people; person	男人 / 女人 / 好人 / 大人 / 中国人 / 美国人 / 日本人
家	home; family	大家 / 家人 / 我家 / 国家 / 老家
友	friend	女友 / 男友 / 朋友 / 好友 / 老友 / 友好

2. 音义

1）将汉字与其相对应的读音和意思连起来。Match the characters with their Pinyin and meanings.

zài	谁	who; whom
jiā	和	be in/at/on
shéi	有	and
hé	在	home; family
yǒu	家	to have

2）用下列汉字组词，比一比，看谁组的词语多。Make words with the following characters — the more, the better.

人：

女：

男：

友：

3）写出下列词语的拼音和意思。Write down the Pinyin and meanings of the following words.

在家__________、__________　　大人__________、__________

有名__________、__________　　家人__________、__________

友好__________、__________　　女孩儿__________、__________

3. 书写

写汉字，注意笔画笔顺。Write the following Chinese characters and pay attention to the stroke order.

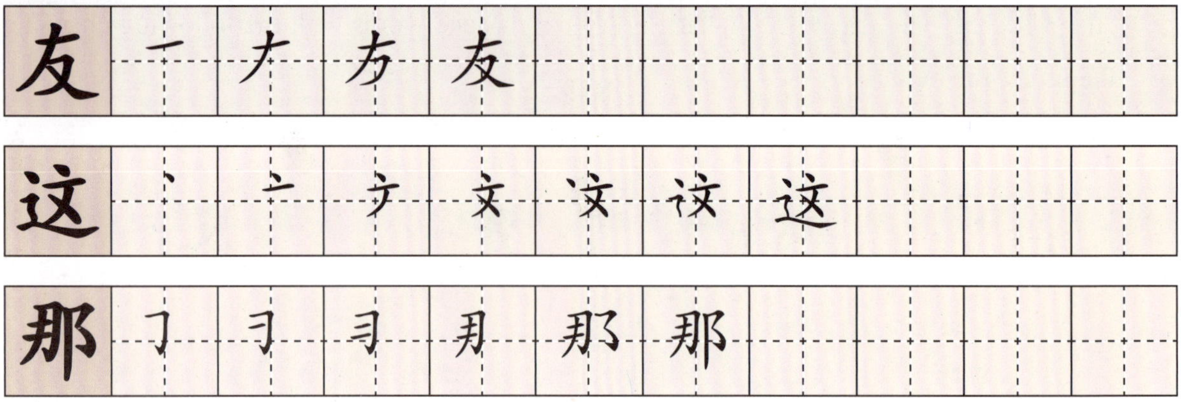

文化知识
Chinese ABC

中国人的亲属称谓

The Forms of Address in A Chinese Family

In the Chinese society, the forms of address in a family make a complicated system to distinguish the age and the blood. For instance, “gēge” and “dìdi” show the age difference, and according to the blood, the paternal grandfather is “yéye” while the maternal grandfather is “wàigōng”.

Moreover, the kinship terms are also extended to social occasions. “Shūshu” is applied to all males of one’s father’s generation, and “āyí” to females of one’s mother’s generation, even though there is no kinship.

Therefore, it is not hard to see what an important role family relationship plays in the Chinese society throughout thousands of years.

Below is an illustration of the “family tree” of the traditional Chinese family.

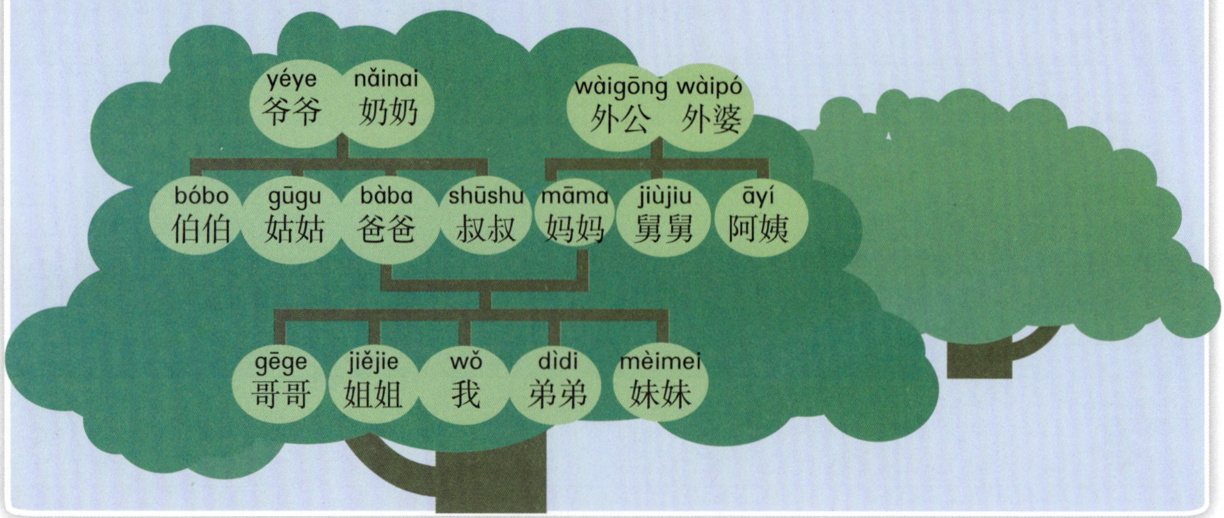

第九课 Lesson 9 你做什么工作？ What do you do?

语言要点

1 用“什么”提问：你做什么工作？

2 “都”的用法：我们都是中文系的学生。

3 量词（一）：个、位

一 课文 | Texts

对话一 你做什么工作？

[Scene] Li Li and Martin meet for the first time.

听录音并朗读
Listen to the recording and read aloud

Lín lǎoshī: Wǒ jièshào yíxià, zhè wèi shì Mǎ Dīng.
林老师：我介绍一下，这位是马丁。
Mǎ Dīng, zhè shì wǒ de péngyou Lǐ Lì.
马丁，这是我的朋友李力。

Lǐ Lì: Nǐ hǎo, Mǎ Dīng! Rènshi nǐ hěn gāoxìng!
李力：你好，马丁！认识你很高兴！

Mǎ Dīng: Nín hǎo! Rènshi nín, wǒ yě hěn gāoxìng.
马丁：您好！认识您，我也很高兴。
Nín yě shì lǎoshī ba?
您也是老师吧？①

Lǐ Lì: Bù, wǒ shì yīshēng. Zhè shì wǒ de míngpiàn.
李力：不，我是医生。这是我的名片。
Nǐ ne? Nǐ zuò shénme gōngzuò?
你呢？你做什么工作？

Mǎ Dīng: Wǒ shì xuésheng.
马丁：我是学生。

Notes

① 您也是老师吧？You are also a teacher, aren't you?
"……吧？"用于表达推测语气。
"……吧？" is used to express a presumption.

位	wèi		(a measure word for person, it is a polite form)
认识	rènshi	*v.*	to know (sb.)
高兴	gāoxìng	*adj.*	happy; glad
吧	ba	*particle*	(used at the end of a sentence to express a presumption)
医生	yīshēng	*n.*	doctor
名片	míngpiàn	*n.*	business card
做	zuò	*v.*	to do
工作	gōngzuò	*n.*	job; work
		v.	to work

对话二　我们都是中文系的学生

[Scene] Tian Yu and Wang Xiaowen are both walking in the campus. Tian Yu drops her book, and Wang Xiaowen picks it up for her.

听录音并朗读
Listen to the recording and read aloud

Wáng Xiǎowén:　Tóngxué,　nǐ　de　shū.
王 小文：同学，你 的 书。①

Tián Yǔ:　Xièxie!　Nǐ　yě　shì　zhège　xuéxiào　de　xuésheng　ba?
田 雨：谢谢！你 也 是 这个 学校 的 学生 吧？

Wáng Xiǎowén:　Duì.　Wǒ　jiào　Wáng Xiǎowén.
王 小文：对。我 叫 王 小文。

Tián Yǔ:　Wǒ　jiào　Tián　Yǔ.　Nǐ　xué　shénme　zhuānyè?
田 雨：我 叫 田 雨。你 学 什么 专业？

Wáng Xiǎowén:　Lìshǐ.　Nǐmen　ne?
王 小文：历史。你们 呢？

Tián Yǔ: Wǒ de zhuānyè shì Zhōngguó wénxué. Zhè shì wǒ de tóngxué,
田雨：我的专业是中国文学。这是我的同学，

wǒmen dōu shì Zhōngwénxì de xuésheng.
我们都是中文系的学生。

Notes

① 同学，你的书。Hi, here is your book.

在中国的学校里，遇到学生模样的陌生人，一般可以称呼为"同学"。When you meet a stranger looking like a student on campus in China, you can address him/her as "同学".

同学	tóngxué	*n.*	classmate; schoolmate
书	shū	*n.*	book
谢谢	xièxie	*v.*	to thank
个	gè		(a measure word used before a noun which does not have a fixed measure word of its own)
学校	xuéxiào	*n.*	school
专业	zhuānyè	*n.*	major
历史	lìshǐ	*n.*	history
中国	Zhōngguó	*n.*	China
文学	wénxué	*n.*	literature
都	dōu	*adv.*	both; all
中文	Zhōngwén	*n.*	Chinese
系	xì	*n.*	department

短文 我学历史专业

听录音、朗读并且复述
Listen to the recording, read aloud, and then retell

Wǒ shì zhège xuéxiào de xuésheng, wǒ xué lìshǐ zhuānyè,
我是这个学校的学生，我学历史专业，
wǒ yǒu hěn duō péngyou. Tāmen shì wǒ de xīn péngyou, tāmen
我有很多朋友。他们是我的新朋友，他们
dōu xué Zhōngguó wénxué, dōu shì Zhōngwénxì de xuésheng.
都学中国文学，都是中文系的学生。
Zhè wèi shì Lǐ Lì, tā bú shì xuésheng, tā shì yīshēng.
这位是李力，他不是学生，他是医生。

多	duō	*adj.*	many; much
新	xīn	*adj.*	new

二 语言要点 | Key points

1 你做什么工作?

先看句子：Read the examples first:

1）她学习<u>什么</u>?	What does she study?
她学习<u>汉语</u>。	She studies Chinese.
2）这是<u>什么</u>书?	What book is this?
这是<u>汉语</u>书。	This is a Chinese book.
3）他做<u>什么工作</u>?	What job does he do?
他是<u>老师</u>。	He is a teacher.
他是<u>医生</u>。	He is a doctor.
他是<u>学生</u>。	He is a student.

如同第八课讲到的，汉语中特殊疑问句的语序与陈述句的语序一致，只需把未知信息换成“什么”、“谁”等疑问代词。

As we mentioned in Lesson 8, in Chinese, the word order of a special question is the same as that of a declarative sentence, only to substitute the unknown part with a question word like "什么", "谁", etc.

▶ 提示 Be aware

在汉语中，问别人工作时经常说"你做什么工作"，但在回答时，经常说"我是……"。
"你做什么工作" is used to ask about sb.'s job, but the answer is usually "我是……"。

2 我们都是中文系的学生。

先看句子：Read the examples first：

1）我们都是学生。 We are both/all students.

2）我和他都有姐姐。 He and I both have elder sisters.

3）他们都学汉语。 They both/all study Chinese.

S + 都 + v.

"都"是副词，表示总括全部，放在动词之前。

In Chinese, the adverb "都" means "both/all", and it should be put in front of the verb.

▶ 提示 Be aware

- 如果句子中同时有"也"和"都"，"也"要放在"都"前面。例如：
  If there are both "也" and "都" in one sentence, "也" should be put in front of "都". For example:
  我是中国人，他们也都是中国人。I am Chinese. They are all Chinese too.

- "不都"和"都不"意义不同。例如：
  "不都" and "都不" have different meanings. For example:
  1）他们都不是中国人。None of them is Chinese.
  2）他们不都是中国人。They are not all Chinese. (Some are Chinese, and some are not.)

3 量词（一）：个、位

1）我有三个好朋友。 I have three good friends.

2）她是一位/个老师。 She is a teacher.

3）这儿有三个学校。 There are three schools here.

4）这位是林老师。 This is Mr. Lin.

5）他也是这个学校的学生。 He is also a student of this school.

Number +	Measure word +	Noun	
一	位	老师	one teacher
三	个	学生	three students

汉语中，数词和名词之间一般会有一个量词。“个”是最常用的量词。很多名词都有专门对应的量词。当数词是“一”时，“一”可以省略，因此，“她是一位/个老师”也可以说成“她是位/个老师”。

In Chinese, there is usually a measure word between a number and a noun. “个” is the most frequently used one. There are many nouns that should match special measure words. When the numeral is “一”, “一” can be omitted. Therefore, “她是一位/个老师” could also be “她是位/个老师”.

三 练习 | Exercises

1. 抢答ABC：听老师的发音，指出是A、B、C中的哪一个。做完后再读一读A、B、C三组，注意三者的区别。Interaction: Listen to the teacher’s pronunciation, and point out the corresponding Pinyin among A, B, and C. Then read aloud all the columns and pay attention to their differences.

A	B	C	A	B	C
jū	zū	zhū	jì	zì	zhì
qù	cù	chù	qī	cī	chī
xú	sú	shú	xī	sī	shī
juān	zuān	zhuān	jiàn	zàn	zhàn
quàn	cuàn	chuàn	jiāng	zāng	zhāng
xuān	suān	shuān	jiào	zào	zhào
jūn	zūn	zhūn	qiǎo	cǎo	chǎo
qūn	cūn	chūn	xiǎo	sǎo	shǎo

2. 听老师的发音，给下列词语标注声调并跟读。Listen to the teacher's pronunciation, mark the tones and read after the teacher.

lüshi lawyer	jingli manager	laoshi teacher	xuesheng student	yisheng doctor
kuaijishi accountant	jiaoshou professor	gongchengshi engineer	yanyuan actor; actress	shangren businessperson

3. 听录音，给下列词语标上声调，然后大声朗读，试试在后续的练习中运用这些词汇。Listen to the recording, mark the tones and read aloud. Try to use these words in the following exercises.

hushi 护士 nurse	daifu 大夫 doctor	siji 司机 driver

jingcha 警察 police	jizhe 记者 reporter; journalist	fuwuyuan 服务员 waiter; waitress

4. 选择填空。Fill in the blanks.

高兴　系　吧　专业　工作　位　个　新　都

1）你做什么________？
2）认识你我也很________。
3）这________学校很好。
4）你们是中国人________？
5）我们________不是中国人。
6）我在中文________学习汉语。
7）我的________是历史。
8）那________是林老师。
9）他们都是我的________朋友。

5. 用“都”改写下面的句子。Paraphrase the following sentences with “都”.

1）我是中国人，他也是中国人。

____

2）我是老师，他也是老师。

____

3）我不是学生，他也不是学生。

____

4）我去美国，他也去美国。

____

5）他学习汉语，她也学习汉语。

____

6. 根据课文完成下面的对话。Complete the conversations according to the texts.

1）林老师：我__________，这位是马丁。马丁，__________。
　　李力：你好！__________！
　　马丁：您好！认识您，我也很高兴。__________？
　　李力：不，我是________。这是我的________。你呢？________？
　　马丁：我是学生，我学习中文。

2）王小文：同学，你的书。
　　田雨：谢谢！你也是__________？
　王小文：对。我叫王小文。
　　田雨：我叫田雨。__________？
　王小文：历史。__________？
　　田雨：我的专业是________。这是我的同学，我们________的学生。

7. 根据课文内容回答问题。Answer the questions according to the texts.

1）李力做什么工作？
2）李力是谁的朋友？
3）马丁是医生吗？
4）田雨学习什么专业？王小文呢？
5）田雨和王小文是一个学校的学生吗？

课堂活动
Activities

1. 介绍一下自己家人的工作。
   Introduce the occupations of your family members.

2. 找一个伙伴，互相询问工作及专业，模仿本课短文，向全班介绍一下你的伙伴。
   Find a partner and ask each other about occupation and major. Then introduce your partner to the class in the form of the passage of this lesson.

四 字、词、句 | Character, word, and sentence

1. 认读

读一读，猜一猜。Read and guess.

做	to do	做什么 / 做好 / 做饭(zuòfàn) / 做生意(shēngyi)
工	work	工人 / 工作 / 工资(gōngzī) / 工厂(gōngchǎng)
个	*measure word*	一个人 / 一个老师 / 一个学生 / 一个学校 / 三个同学 / 四个朋友
位	*measure word*	这位老师 / 那位同学 / 一位老人 / 一位医生
的	*particle*	我的书 / 他的老师 / 她的男朋友 / 谁的学生 / 我的工作
文	(written) language	中文 / 文字 / 英文 / 法文 / 日文 / 文学 / 文化 (wénhuà)
新	new	新同学 / 新朋友 / 新书 / 新学校 / 新老师 / 新工作
书	book	汉语书 / 中文书 / 英语书 / 新书 / 好书 / 书名 / 我的书
中	Chinese inside; in the middle	中国 / 中文 手中 / 水中 / 书中 / 心中 / 家中 / 中学

2. 音义

1）将汉字与其相对应的读音和意思连起来。Match the characters with their Pinyin and meanings.

gōng	做	book
zuò	书	to do
xīn	工	new
shū	新	work

2）用下列汉字组词，比一比，看谁组的词语多。Make words with the following characters—the more, the better.

的：　新：　个：　工：　中：

3）写出下列词语的拼音和意思。Write down the Pinyin and meanings of the following words.

工人 ____________、____________　　中学 ____________、____________

文化 ____________、____________　　工资 ____________、____________

心中 ____________、____________　　书名 ____________、____________

3. 书写

写汉字，注意笔画笔顺。Write the following Chinese characters and pay attention to the stroke order.

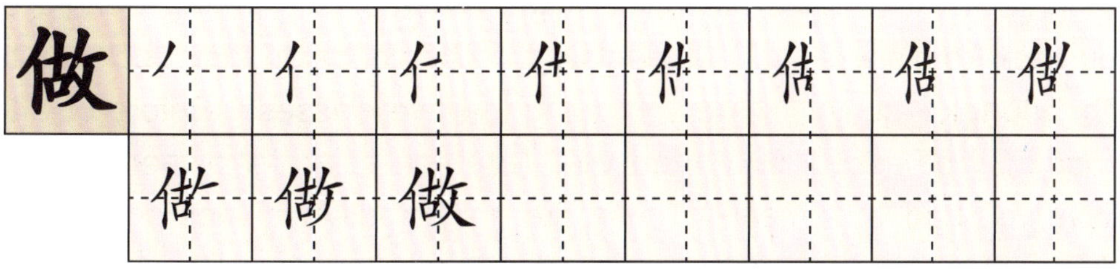

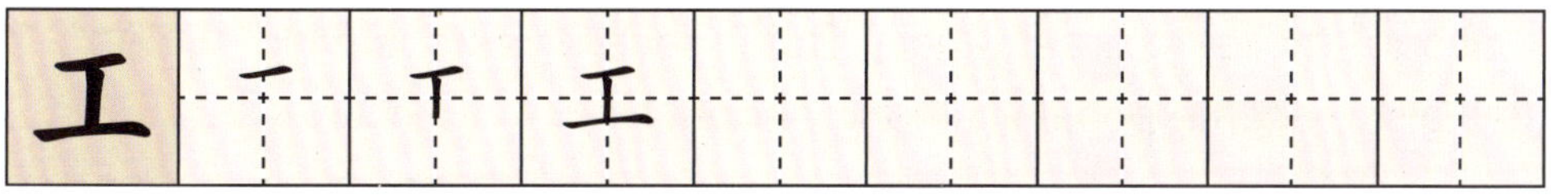

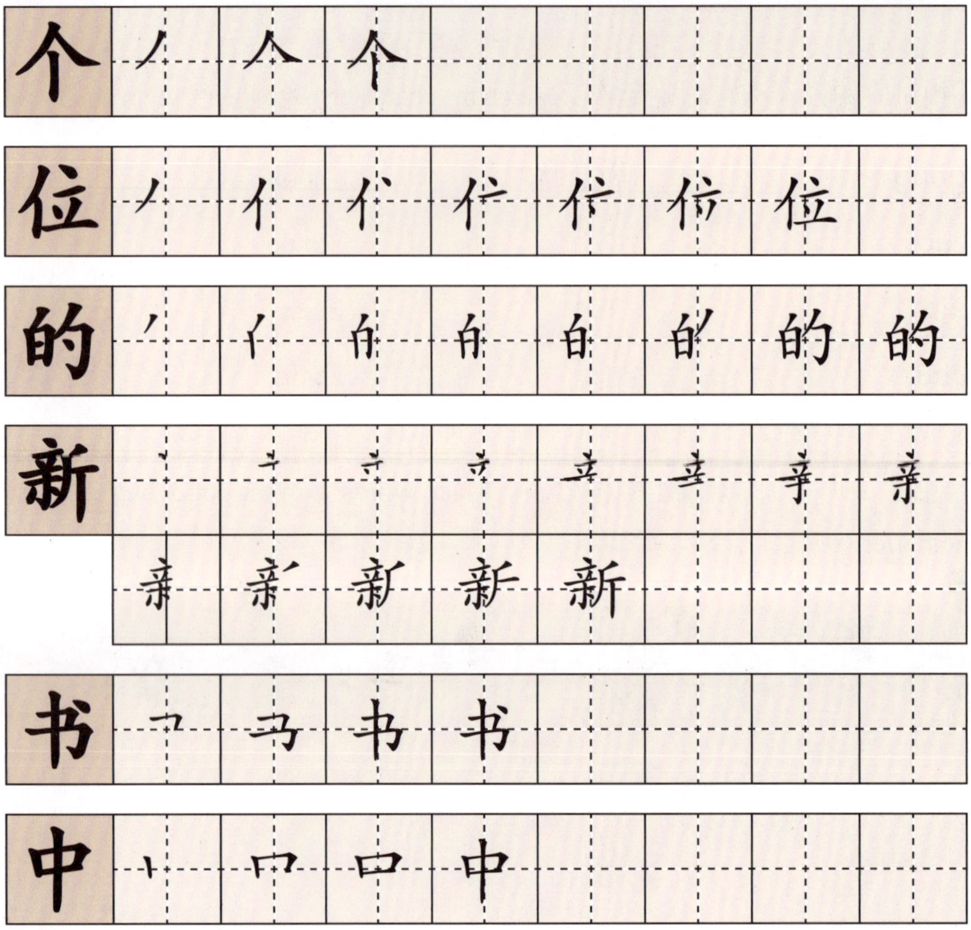

文化知识
Chinese ABC

打招呼
Greetings

The way that Chinese people greet each other is quite different from that in the West. The Chinese people tend to confine the discussion to the matter (they often ask about specific things as greetings). For example, seeing somebody going out, they may say “Chūqù ɑ?” (Are you going out?) or “Qù nǎ ɑ?” (Where are you going?) People coming back with bags of shopping might be greeted with “Mǎi dōngxi qù lɑ?” (Are you back from shopping?) Students with schoolbags on their back can be inquired with “Shàngkè qù yɑ?” (Are you going to have classes?) Before or after the meals, one may be asked “Qù chīfàn yɑ?” (Are you going for dinner?) or “Chī le mɑ?” (Have you had your meal?) These are not actually inquiries on people’s whereabouts or action plans but just ways of greeting. In the past, Chinese people seldom say “nǐ hǎo” (hello) to greet others. But in recent years, saying “nǐ hǎo”, “hi” and “hello” has also become popular among people.

第十课 Lesson 10

苹果多少钱一斤？ How much are the apples?

语言要点

1 1—100的基本数词

2 人民币的写法和读法

3 “太 + adj. + 了”：太贵了！

4 “几”和“多少”

一 课文 | Texts

对话一 您买什么？

[Scene] At a bakery.

听录音并朗读
Listen to the recording and read aloud

A： Qǐngwèn nín mǎi shénme?
A：请问 您 买 什么？
B： Wǒ mǎi miànbāo.
B：我 买 面包。
A： Mǎi jǐ gè?
A：买 几 个？
B： Liǎng gè. Yígòng duōshao qián?
B： 两 个。一共 多少 钱？
A： Wǔ kuài.
A：五 块。
B： Gěi nín qián.
B：给 您 钱。

买	mǎi	*v.*	to buy
面包	miànbāo	*n.*	bread
几	jǐ	*num.*	how many; how much (less than 10)
两	liǎng	*num.*	two
一共	yīgòng	*adv.*	altogether; in all
多少	duōshao	*pron.*	how many; how much
钱	qián	*n.*	money
五	wǔ	*num.*	five
块	kuài		(a measure word) piece; chunk; yuan (for money)
给	gěi	*v.*	to give

对话二 苹果多少钱一斤？

[Scene] At a market.

听录音并朗读
Listen to the recording and read aloud

A： Qǐngwèn, píngguǒ duōshao qián yì jīn?
A：请问，苹果多少钱一斤？
B： Sì kuài wǔ.
B：四块五。
A： Tài guì le! Piányi yìdiǎnr ba.
A：太贵了！便宜一点儿吧。
B： Hǎo ba, sì kuài yì jīn, nín mǎi duōshao?
B：好吧①，四块一斤，您买多少？
A： Wǔ gè.
A：五个。
B： Nín hái yào shénme?
B：您还要什么？
A： Xièxie, bú yào le. Duōshao qián?
A：谢谢，不要了。多少钱？
B： Liù kuài sì.
B：六块四。

Notes

① 好吧。OK.
表示同意，意思同英语中的“OK; alright”。
“好吧”, like “OK; alright” in English, indicates consent.

苹果	píngguǒ	*n.*	apple
斤	jīn		(a measure word) half a kilogram
四	sì	*num.*	four
太	tài	*adv.*	extremely; too
贵	guì	*adj.*	expensive
便宜	piányi	*adj.*	cheap
一点儿	yīdiǎnr		a bit; a little
吧	ba	*particle*	(used at the end of an imperative sentence to soften the tone or used at the end of a sentence to indicate consent or approval)
还	hái	*adv.*	even more; also
要	yào	*v.*	want; need
六	liù	*num.*	six

短文 今天我很高兴

听录音、朗读并且复述
Listen to the recording, read aloud, and then retell

Jīntiān wǒ hěn gāoxìng, mǎi le yì běn Hànyǔ shū、liǎng gè miànbāo,
今天我很高兴，买了一本汉语书、两个面包，
háiyǒu wǔ gè píngguǒ. Píngguǒ sì kuài qián yì jīn, miànbāo liǎng kuài wǔ yí
还有五个苹果。苹果四块钱一斤，面包两块五一
gè, Hànyǔ shū shí' èr kuài, yígòng èrshísān kuài sì, bú tài guì.
个，汉语书十二块，一共二十三块四，不太贵。

今天	jīntiān	*n.*	today
了	le	*particle*	(used after a verb to indicate the completion of an action)
本	běn		(a measure word for books, dictionaries, magazines, etc.)
十二	shí' èr	*num.*	twelve
二十三	èrshísān	*num.*	twenty-three

二 语言要点 | Key points

1 1—100的基本数词

1 yī 一	2 èr 二	3 sān 三	4 sì 四	5 wǔ 五	6 liù 六	7 qī 七	8 bā 八	9 jiǔ 九	10 shí 十
11 shíyī 十一	12 shí' èr 十二	13 shísān 十三	14 shísì 十四	15 shíwǔ 十五	16 shíliù 十六	17 shíqī 十七	18 shíbā 十八	19 shíjiǔ 十九	20 èrshí 二十
21 èrshíyī 二十一	22 èrshí' èr 二十二	23 èrshísān 二十三	24 èrshísì 二十四	25 èrshíwǔ 二十五	26 èrshíliù 二十六	27 èrshíqī 二十七	28 èrshíbā 二十八	29 èrshíjiǔ 二十九	30 sānshí 三十
100 yībǎi 一百									

2 人民币的写法和读法

汉语中钱数的表达单位 The units of RMB

RMB	Spoken	Written
Basic unit	块 kuài	元 yuán
1/10 yuan	毛 máo	角 jiǎo
1/100 yuan	分 fēn	分 fēn

人民币的读法 How to count in RMB

	Spoken	Written
¥0.2	两毛（钱）	两角
¥1.0	一块（钱）	一元
¥2.5	两块五（毛）	两元五角
¥2.52	两块五毛二（分）	两元五角二分
¥22.6	二十二块六（毛）	二十二元六角
¥25.05	二十五块零 (líng zero) 五分	二十五元零五分
¥120.0	一百二十块	一百二十元
¥112.0	一百一十二块	一百一十二元
¥102.4	一百零二块四（毛）	一百零二元四角
¥202.0	二百零二块 两百零二块	二百零二元
¥500.4	五百块零四毛	五百元零四角

▶ 提示 Be aware

- 口语中，钱数有两个或两个以上单位时，最后的“毛”或“分”一般可以省略。但是，如果单位“毛”或“分”直接在“零”后面，那么“毛”或“分”不能省略。例如：

  When there are two or more units of a sum of money, usually the “毛” or “分” in the end can be omitted. But, if the unit “毛” or “分” is right behind “零”, it cannot be omitted. For example:

两块五（毛）　　两块五毛二（分）
二十五块零五分　　五百块零四毛

♦ 数字“2”可以读“二”，也可以读“两（liǎng）”。直接读数字时，“2”读作“二”。例如：“1、2、3”读作“一、二、三”，“25”读作“二十五”。

In Chinese, 2 can be pronounced as “èr” or “liǎng”. In numbers, “2” is read as “èr”. For example, “1, 2, 3” is read as “yī, èr, sān”, and “25” is read as “èrshíwǔ”.

但在度量衡单位量词前，“二”和“两”常常可以通用。例如：

When used before a measure word of length, capacity or weight, “2” can be read as either “èr” or “liǎng”. For example:

2斤苹果　　èr/liǎng jīn píngguǒ

在一般量词前面时，要读“两”。例如：

When used before other measure words, “2” is generally read as “liǎng”. For example:

2本书　　liǎng běn shū
2个苹果　　liǎng gè píngguǒ
2块面包　　liǎng kuài miànbāo

3 太贵了！

先看句子：Read the examples first:

1）这本书太好了！　　This book is very good!
2）他们太忙了！　　They are too busy!
3）今天我太高兴了！　　I'm very happy today!

“太 + adj. + 了！”意思是“...too...!”或“...very...!”表示程度极高或超过可接受的程度。既可以表达积极意义，也可以表达消极意义。

“太 + adj. + 了!” means “...too...!” or “...very...!”, indicating a degree extremely high or even unacceptably high. This pattern can express both desirable and undesirable meanings.

4 “几”和“多少”

先看句子，注意“几”和“多少”的不同之处：

Read the examples first, pay attention to the difference between “几” and “多少”:

1）你有几本书？/你有多少（本）书？ How many books do you have?

2）你买几斤？/你买多少（斤）？ How many/much do you want?

3）你有几个学生？/你有多少（个）学生？ How many students do you have?

“几”和“多少”都可以询问数量。一般来说，估计被问的数量在10以下时，用“几”提问，后面必须带量词；估计在10以上或难以估计时用“多少”，后面可不带量词。

“几” and “多少” are both for quantity inquiry. Usually, when the inquirer estimates that the number is less than 10, he would ask with “几” which must be followed by a measure word; while if the number is estimated above 10 or is hard to estimate, “多少” is used, after which measure words are optional.

提示 Be aware

问钱数时，一般用“多少钱？”来提问。

“多少钱？” is often used when asking for the amount of money.

三 练习 | Exercises

1. 听录音，跟读数词。Read after the recording for the numbers.

2. 听录音，写出拼音并朗读，注意“一”的变调。Listen to the recording, fill in the blanks and read aloud. Pay attention to the sandhi of “一”.

yì______bǐ	yì______shuǐ	yì______dāo	yì______shū
yí______zì	yí______shì	yí______qián	yí______yào

3. 听录音，给下列词语标上声调，然后大声朗读，试试在后续的练习中运用这些词汇。Listen to the recording, mark the tones and read aloud. Try to use these words in the following exercises.

毛 mao	分 fen	元 yuan	角 jiao
零 ling	二 er	三 san	六 liu
七 qi	八 ba	九 jiu	十 shi
 西瓜 xigua	 香蕉 xiangjiao	 葡萄 putao	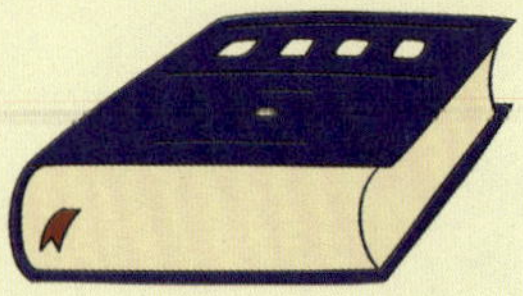 词典 cidian

4. 听录音，用阿拉伯数字写出钱数。Write down the amounts of money in Arabic numerals according to the recording.

______元　______元　______元　______元　______元

______元　______元　______元　______元　______元

5. 读下面的绕口令，比一比，看谁读得又快又好。Read the tongue twister below. The more accurate and faster, the better.

四是四，十是十，十四是十四，四十是四十。

四不是十，十也不是四，十四不是四十，四十也不是十四。

6. 词语替换。Substitute the underlined parts in the sentences with the given words and expressions.

1）太贵了。	大　小　好　白　忙　便宜
2）我买两斤苹果。	一个西瓜　两本书　一本词典
3）苹果多少钱一斤？	西瓜　香蕉
4）给您钱。	书　词典　面包　苹果

7. 写出下列名词所对应的量词。Write down the measure words for the following nouns.

三______苹果　两______书　两______医生　五______面包

三______学生　　一______西瓜　　一______人　　两______钱

8. 选择填空。Fill in the blanks.

1）你买________个面包？
2）你有________本书？
3）你有________个弟弟？
4）你们学校有________学生？

几
多少

9. 根据图示回答问题。Answer the questions according to the pictures.

1）

2）

3）

4）

10. 完成下列对话。Complete the following conversations.

1）A：＿＿＿＿＿＿＿＿＿＿＿＿？

B：我买面包。＿＿＿＿＿＿＿＿＿＿＿＿？

A：两块五。＿＿＿＿＿＿＿＿＿＿＿＿？

B：三个。

2）A：＿＿＿＿＿＿＿＿＿＿＿＿？

B：不要了，谢谢。＿＿＿＿＿＿＿＿＿＿＿＿？

A：一共十五块钱。

11. 翻译下列句子。Translation.

1）What can I do for you?

2）How much are the apples?

3）What else do you want?

4）How much for all of these?

5）Thirty yuan and eighty fen for the two books.

6）Here is the money.

课堂活动 Activities

1. 老师随意列举1—100中的一个阿拉伯数字，让学生读出，看谁读得又快又准确。

   The teacher shows numbers from 1—100 randomly and lets students read them out. Compete for accuracy and speed.

2. 老师将学生分成两组，然后读数字，请不同组的两个学生分别写在黑板上，同组内学生轮流书写，写完后比比看哪一组写得又快又准。

   Divide the students into two groups. Students from different groups write down numbers read by the teacher on the blackboard in turn (two students each time). The group that is faster and more accurate wins.

3. 教师出示写有钱数的卡片，或者展示商品标签照片，请学生读出钱数。

   The teacher demonstrates cards with sums of money on or pictures of price tags, and asks the students to read the amounts aloud.

4. 和你的同桌模仿对话二，分角色练习买水果的对话，试试买别的水果。

   Do the role play with your deskmate taking Dialogue 2 as an example. Try buying some other fruits.

5. 下课后去商店买一些你需要的东西，第二天向全班报告你买的东西和价钱。

   Go shopping after class and report the stuff you buy and their prices to the class the next day.

四 字、词、句 | Character, word, and sentence

1. 认读

读一读，猜一猜。Read and guess.

买	to buy	买什么 / 买苹果 / 买书 / 不买 / 买多少 / 买几斤
两	two	两个 / 两块 / 两毛钱 / 两本书 / 两个人 / 两天 / 两位
斤	half a kilogram	两斤 / 四斤 / 公斤 (gōngjīn) / 十斤米
果	fruit	苹果 / 水果
本	*measure word*	一本书 / 一本词典
钱	money	几块钱 / 十块钱 / 多少钱 / 有钱 / 零钱 / 我的钱 / 很多钱
给	to give	给他 / 给钱 / 给你钱 / 给我书 / 不要给他
要	want + n. want + to do	不要 / 要什么 / 要钱 / 要多少 你要买什么？/ 我要问一下爸爸。/ 他要来中国。/ 我要学习汉语。
多	many; much	多少 / 很多 / 不多 / 太多了
少	few; little	很少 / 不少 / 太少了

2. 音义

1）将汉字与其相对应的读音和意思连起来。Match the characters with their Pinyin and meanings.

yào	买	fruit
guǒ	要	to buy
qián	给	want
gěi	果	money
mǎi	两	to give
liǎng	钱	two

2）用下列汉字组词，比一比，看谁组的词语多。Make words with the following characters — the more, the better.

果：

钱：

斤：

两：

要：

买：

本：

给：

3）比较一下两个汉字的不同，并标注拼音。Find out the difference between each pair of characters and write down the Pinyin of them.

木　本

字　学

白　百

明　朋

大　太

小　少

吗　妈

他　她

3. 书写

写汉字，注意笔画笔顺。Write the following Chinese characters and pay attention to the stroke order.

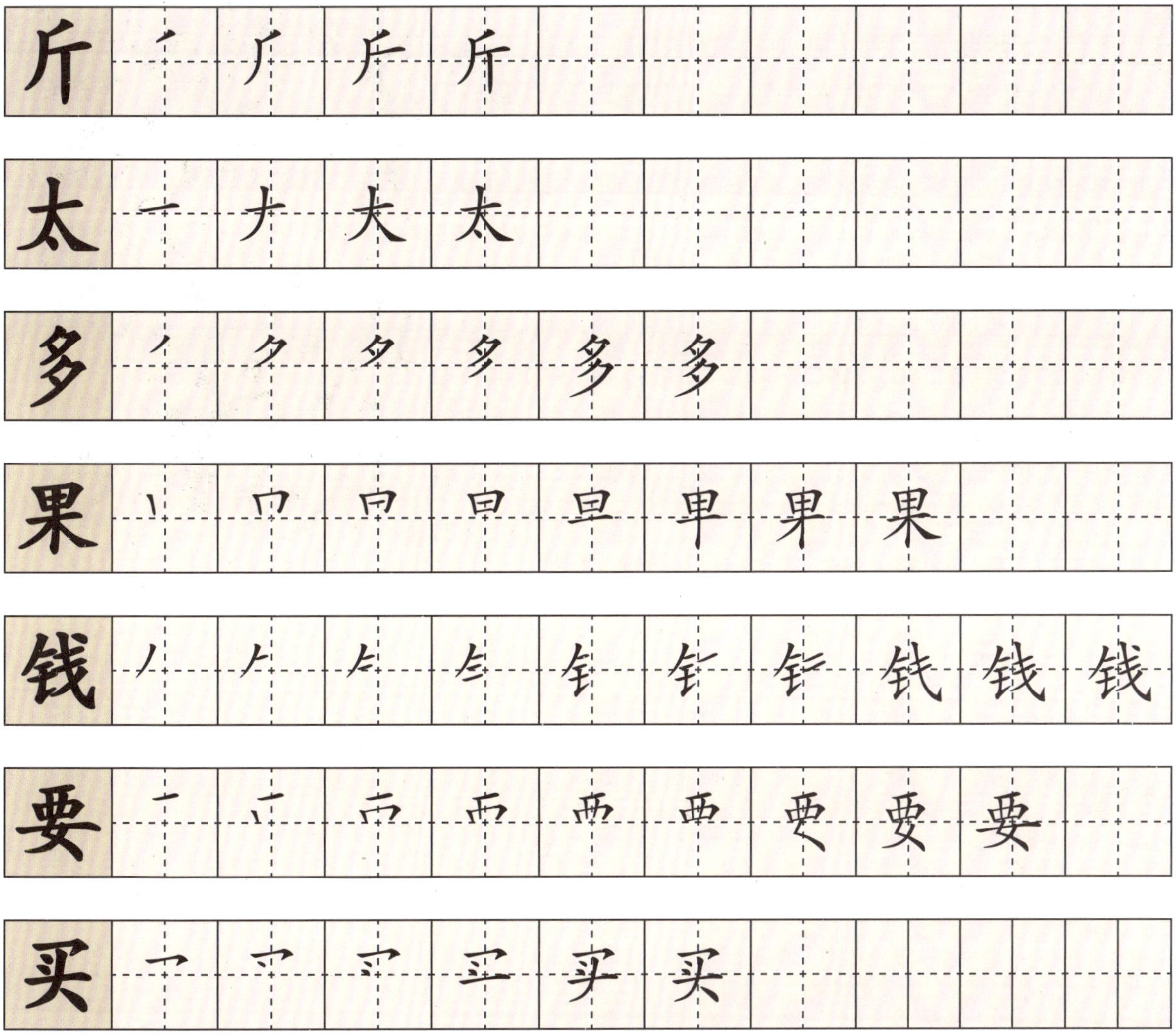

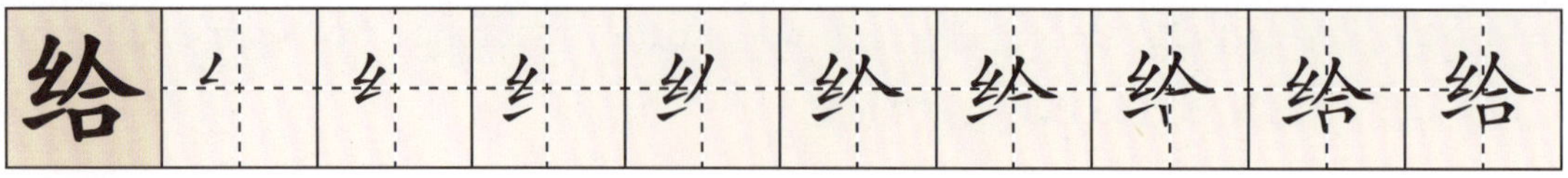

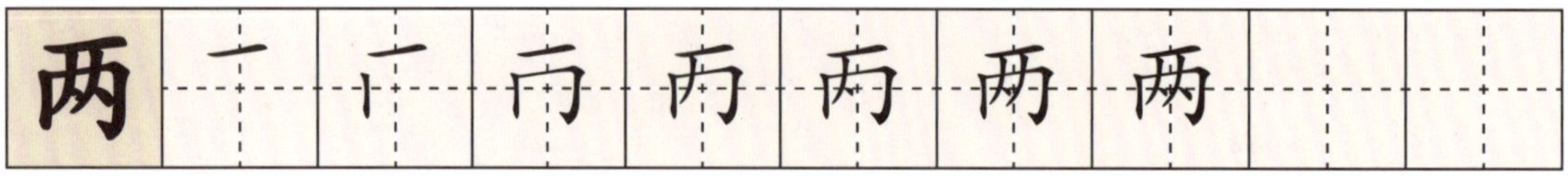

文化知识

Chinese ABC

中国的货币

Chinese Currency

China is one of the first countries that used shells as currency. Since the Shang Dynasty, Chinese people started to make coins of bronze, which are the earliest metal currency in the world. Currency of ensuing dynasties was mainly made of copper and iron, and currency made of silver became popular starting from the Ming Dynasty. At the early time currency was coined round, square, or in the shape of knife and spade. Gradually round coins became popular. In the center of a round coin, there is a square hole for lining up. Moreover, China is also one of the first countries where paper currency is used. According to some historical records, "jiaozi"(交子) in the North Song Dynasty is the oldest paper money in the world.

课文英文翻译
English translation of the texts

第六课

Dialogue 1 Hello!

Wang Xiaowen: Hello!
Martin: Hello!
Wang Xiaowen: Excuse me, what's your name?
Martin: My name is Martin. And you are?
Wang Xiaowen: I'm Wang Xiaowen.

Dialogue 2 Are you busy?

Daming: Are you busy?
Martin: Very busy. How about you?
Daming: I'm not busy.
Martin: How are your parents doing?
Daming: They are doing well.

Short Passage

She is Wang Xiaowen. She's very busy. What about you? What's your name? Are you busy?

第七课

Dialogue 1 May I know your surname?

Martin: Sir, excuse me, may I know your surname?
Mr. Lin: My surname is Lin.
Martin: How do you do, Mr. Lin?
Mr. Lin: How do you do? What's your name?
Martin: My name is Martin.
Mr. Lin: Which country are you from?
Martin: I'm American.

Dialogue 2 Allow me to introduce you to each other.

Martin: Hello, Mr. Lin. Let me introduce you to each other. This is my friend Daming.
Mr. Lin: (to Daming) How do you do?
Daming: How do you do, Mr. Lin?
Mr. Lin: Do you also learn Chinese?

Daming:	Yes, I do.
Mr. Lin:	Are you also American?
Daming:	I'm not American. I'm British.

Short Passage

Hello, everyone. Let me introduce myself. My name is Martin. I'm American. I am a student and I study Chinese. This is my friend. His name is Daming. He is British. He learns Chinese too.

第八课

Dialogue 1　Who is she?

Wang Xiaowen:	Is this your family photo?
Martin:	Yes. This is my dad, this is my mum, this is my younger sister, and that is my younger brother.
Wang Xiaowen:	Who is she?
Martin:	She is my girlfriend.
Wang Xiaowen:	She is pretty. Which country is she from?
Martin:	She is also American.

Dialogue 2　Do you have elder brothers or elder sisters?

Wang Xiaowen:	Martin, do you have elder brothers or elder sisters?
Martin:	I have an elder brother, no elder sisters. How about you?
Wang Xiaowen:	I have neither elder brothers nor elder sisters.
Martin:	My dad, mum, younger brother and younger sister are in the U.S.A. My elder brother is in Japan. He studies Japanese.

Short passage

Hi, everyone. I am Martin. I'm American. Now I am in China. I study Chinese. My girlfriend is American too. She is very beautiful. She also learns Chinese. My dad, mum, younger brother and younger sister are in the U.S.A. My elder brother is in Japan. He studies Japanese.

第九课

Dialogue 1　What do you do?

Mr. Lin:	Let me introduce. This is Martin. Martin, this is my friend Li Li.
Li Li:	Hi, Martin. Nice to meet you.
Martin:	Hello. Nice to meet you too. You are also a teacher, aren't you?
Li Li:	No, I am a doctor. Here is my business card. How about you? What do you do?
Martin:	I am a student.

Dialogue 2 We are both students from the Chinese Department.

Wang Xiaowen: Hi, here is your book.
Tian Yu: Thank you. You are also a student of this school, right?
Wang Xiaowen: Yes. My name is Wang Xiaowen.
Tian Yu: I'm Tian Yu. What do you study?
Wang Xiaowen: History. And you?
Tian Yu: My major is Chinese literature. This is my classmate. We are both students from the Chinese Department.

Short passage

I am a student of this school. I major in history. I have a lot of friends. They are my new friends. They all study Chinese literature. All of them are students from the Chinese Department.

This is Li Li. He is not a student. He is a doctor.

第十课

Dialogue 1 What would you like to buy?

A: Excuse me, what would you like to buy?
B: Bread.
A: How much do you want?
B: Two loaves. How much altogether?
A: Five yuan.
B: Here's the money.

Dialogue 2 How much are the apples?

A: Excuse me, how much are the apples?
B: Four yuan fifty fen per jin.
A: It's too expensive! Can I have it at a lower price?
B: OK, four yuan per jin. How many do you want?
A: Five apples.
B: What else do you want?
A: Nothing, thanks. How much?
B: Six forty.

Short passage

I am very happy today. I bought a Chinese book, two loaves of bread, and five apples. The apples are four yuan per jin, the bread is two yuan fifty fen each loaf, and the Chinese book is twelve yuan. Altogether they cost twenty-three yuan forty fen — not very expensive.

练习答案

Answers to exercises

第一课

随堂练

一、韵母

□ 随堂练P5

2. 听老师的发音，写下韵母，并跟读。Listen to the teacher, write down the finals, and read after the teacher.

   o　ou　ü　i　ei　e　a　ao　ai　u

3. 辨别对错。指出老师的发音是对的还是错的，如果是错的，请说出正确的发音。（教师发括号中的音。）True/False. Tell true or false about the teacher's pronunciation and correct the wrong ones.

   o（ou）　i（ü）　a（ai）　e（ei）　u（u）　ü（ü）

   ou（o）　ei（ei）　ao（ou）　ai（ao）

□ 随堂练P6

1. 听老师的发音，写下韵母，并跟读。Listen to the teacher, write down the finals, and read after the teacher.

   eng　en　ong　an　ang

2. 辨别对错。指出老师的发音是对的还是错的，如果是错的，请说出正确的发音。（教师发括号中的音。）True/False. Tell true or false about the teacher's pronunciation and correct the wrong ones.

   ong（ang）　en（en）　ang（eng）　eng（ang）　an（ang）

二、声母

□ 随堂练P8

听录音，看图片，填出声母。Listen to the recording, look at the pictures, and fill in the initials.

m̲āo　m̲ā　m̲ō　n̲ǎin̲ai　f̲ēi　l̲ā

☐ 随堂练P9

1. 听老师的发音，写下声母，并跟读。Listen to the teacher, write down the initials, and read after the teacher.

bo, po	mo, fo	de, te	le, ne
ge, ke	bi, pi	la, na	hu, fu
bai, mai	nei, lei	pao, bao	fou, hou
kan, kang	gen, geng	heng, hong	

2. 辨别对错。指出老师的发音是对的还是错的，如果是错的，请说出正确的发音。（教师发括号中的音。）True/False. Tell true or false about the teacher's pronunciation and correct the wrong ones.

bu（pu）	dai（tai）	da（da）	gai（kai）
tou（dou）	ke（he）	ta（ta）	ku（gu）

三、声调

☐ 随堂练P13

2. 听老师朗读拼音，标出声调。Listen to the teacher and mark the tones.

dǎ　lù　gāi　mèi　lǎo　hòu　hěn　hóng

dàhóng　dàlóu　hóngdēng　hēibǎn　hěngāo

练习

4. 听老师的发音，写下声母，并注意每组发音的区别。Listen to the teacher, write down the initials and differentiate the similar pronunciations in each pair.

bǎo	pǎo	bí	pí	bú	pú	bēng	pēng
dài	tài	duó	tuó	dǐng	tǐng	dōu	tōu
gōng	kōng	gè	kè	gǔ	kǔ	gàn	kàn
bǎn	bǎng	cān	cāng	pén	péng	gēn	gēng

5. 听录音填写声母。Listen to the recording and fill in the initials.

bāngmáng　kěnéng　pífū　líkāi

gǔdài　fādá　tàidù　hēibǎn

6. 听录音填写韵母和声调。Listen to the recording and fill in the finals and tones.

nǚrén　　shànghǎi　　zǒulù　　láolèi

dōngfāng　　hěnhǎo　　měimèng　　hēchá

第二课

随堂练

一、韵母

□ 随堂练P21

1. 请将下面的韵母写成独立的音节。Respell the finals below as independent syllables.

ian — yan　　ing — ying　　iong — yong　　uo — wo　　uai — wai

ueng — weng　　üe — yue　　üan — yuan　　ün — yun

2. 将下面的声母、韵母拼合起来。Combine the following initials and finals.

d + iou → diu　　h + uei → hui　　l + iou → liu　　k + uen → kun

d + uei → dui　　t + uen → tun　　n + iou → niu　　g + uei → gui

二、声母

□ 随堂练P24

2. 听老师的发音，写下声母，并跟读。Listen to the teacher, write down the initials, and read after the teacher.

zài　cāo　cén　zǎn　sòng　cáng

zū　cùn　suī　zèng　cuò　suàn

□ 随堂练P27

1. 将下面的声母、韵母拼合起来。Combine the initials and finals below.

j + üan → juan　　l + üe → lüe　　q + ün → qun　　x + üan → xuan

3. 辨别对错。指出老师的发音是对的还是错的，如果是错的，请说出正确的发音。（教师发括号中的音。）True/False. Tell true or false about the teacher's pronunciation and correct the wrong ones.

zhī（zī）　　chè（chì）　　qǐ（qǐ）　　xì（sì）　　jǐ（zhǐ）

shā (chā)　　ruò (ruò)　　zòu (còu)　　cái (chái)　　sū (sī)

4. 听老师的发音，标出你听到的拼音。（教师读标有下划线的音节。）Listen to the teacher and mark the Pinyin you hear.

jí — qí　　zhù — chù　　zá — zhá

zēng — zhēng — jīng　　cī — chī — qī　　sù — shù — xù

三、声调

□ 随堂练P29

听录音，标声调。Listen to the recording and mark the tones.

jiā	huà	wán	quán	liù	duì	wěn	qián
qǐng	yuè	luò	hóu	tūn	liǎng	diū	tuǐ
tái	pǎo	biǎo	mèng				

练习

6. 听录音填写声母，然后跟读。Listen to the recording, fill in the initials, and read aloud.

j iā	zh ù	ch ǎng	zh ēn	s ī	c ì
q iào	j ué	ch ún	j iě	ch uī	s uàn
zh uǎn	sh ǔn	z ǔ	x ián	j iǒng	x iāng

7. 听录音填写韵母和声调，然后跟读。Listen to the recording, fill in the finals and tones, and read aloud.

xié	xué	xiān	jiāng	jiào	jù
qǔ	qún	qīn	huī	diū	kuà
dōu	zhuài	shùn	chuāng	duō	luàn

第三课

汉字练习

2. 根据所学内容写出下列字符和图画所对应的现代汉字。Write down the modern characters corresponding to the following pictographs and pictures.

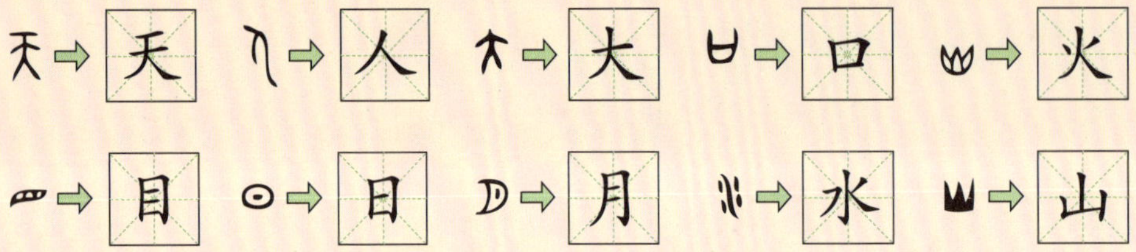

3．根据笔画数为下列汉字归类。Classify the characters according to the number of strokes.

2 strokes：人

3 strokes：大、口、山

4 strokes：天、火、日、月、水

5 strokes：目

4．将汉字与其相对应的读音连起来。Match the characters with their Pinyin.

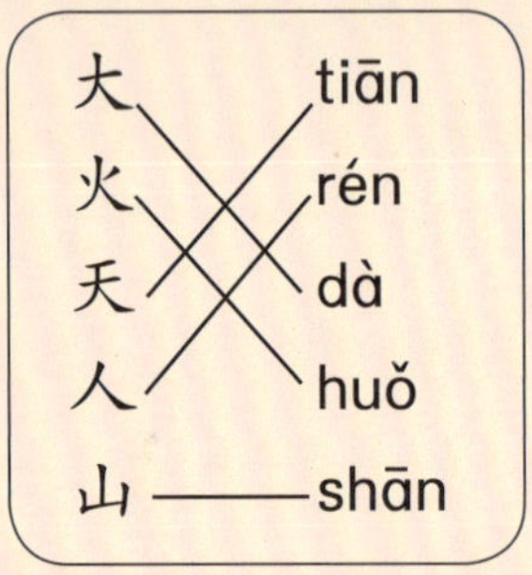

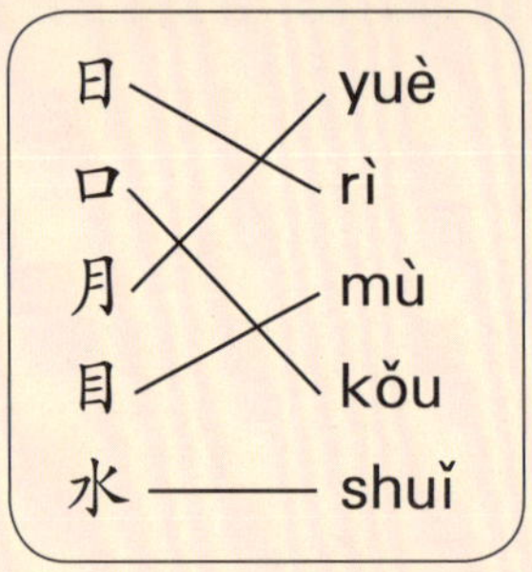

5．从本课所学的汉字中，找出带有下面笔画的汉字。Find out the characters learned in this lesson that are with the following strokes.

丶：火

一：大、天、日、口、月、目

丨：山、日、口、目

亅：水

丿：人、大、天、火、月、水

㇏：人、大、天、火、水

㇕：口、日、目

𠃌：月

语音练习

2．听录音，标出每个音节的声调。Listen to the recording and mark the tone of each syllable.

yī	èr	sān	sì	wǔ	liù	qī	bā	jiǔ	shí
一	二	三	四	五	六	七	八	九	十

3．听录音填写声母。Listen to the recording and fill in the initials.

zhōngguó	běijīng	shànghǎi	guǎngzhōu
xī'ān	xuéxiào	jiàoshì	cāntīng
túshūguǎn	wèishēngjiān		

4．听录音填写韵母和声调。Listen to the recording and fill in the finals and tones.

zuòyè	kànshū	rìlì	shàngwǔ
míngtiān	wǎngqiú	yóuyǒng	pǎobù
duànliàn	yùndòng		

第四课

汉字练习

2．根据所学内容写出下列字符和图画所对应的现代汉字。Write down the modern characters corresponding to the following pictographs and pictures.

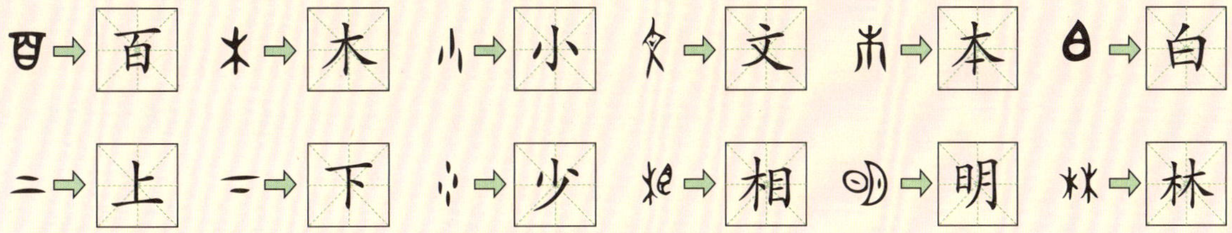

3．根据笔画数为下列汉字归类。Classify the characters according to the number of strokes.

3 strokes：小、上、下　　4 strokes：文、木、少

5 strokes：本、白　　6 strokes：百

8 strokes：林、泪、明　　9 strokes：相

4．将汉字与其相对应的读音连起来。Match the characters with their Pinyin.

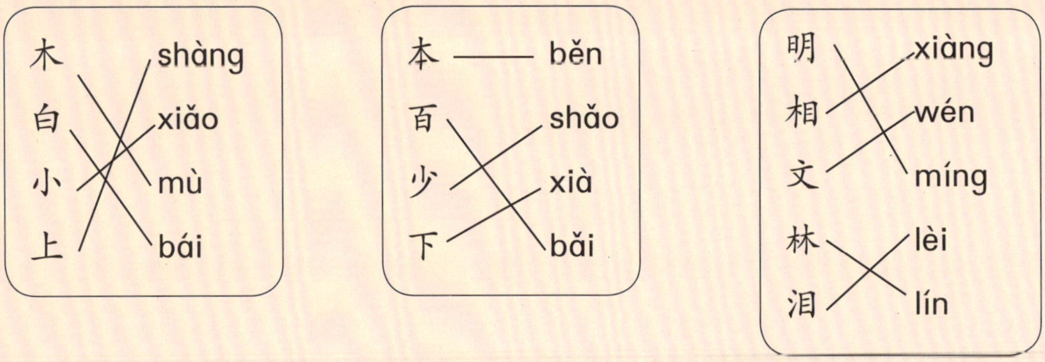

语音练习

1．在空白处写出听到的拼音，了解一下中国人的家庭关系。Write down the Pinyin in the blanks according to what you hear and learn about the family relationship of Chinese people.

1）yéye	2）nǎinai	3）bàba	4）māma	5）shūshu
6）gūgu	7）jiějie	8）mèimei	9）gēge	10）dìdi

2．听录音，标出第一个音节的声调。Listen to the recording and mark the tone of the first syllable in each word.

bàba	māma	gēge	jiějie	dìdi	mèimei
érzi	pánzi	kuàizi	zhēn de	hǎo de	nǐ de
wǒmen	nǐmen	lái ba	zǒu ba	chīle	shuìle
tóufa	dōngxi	nàme	yuǎn ma	kèqi	xièxie

3．听录音填空。Fill in the blanks according to the recording.

mùgōng	shūběn	báisè	èrbǎi
xiǎoshuō	shàonián	shàngchē	xiàqu
míngliàng	xìnglín	xiàngqí	yǎnlèi
érzi	sūnzi	shítou	zhěntou
ěrduo	péngyou	xuésheng	wǒmen

4．听录音，写句子。Listen to the recording and write down the sentences in Pinyin.

1）Qǐng gēn wǒ dú.

2）Qǐng tīng wǒ shuō.

3）Qǐng zài shuō yí cì.

4）Rúguǒ nǐ yǒu wèntí, qǐng wèn wǒ.

第五课

汉字练习

2. 根据所学内容写出下列字符和图画所对应的现代汉字。Write down the modern characters corresponding to the following pictographs and pictures.

 ⇨ 刀  ⇨ 力  ⇨ 米  ⇨ 来  ⇨ 心  ⇨ 田  ⇨ 手

 ⇨ 好  ⇨ 女  ⇨ 子 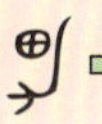 ⇨ 男  ⇨ 想  ⇨ 门 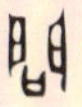 ⇨ 问

3. 根据笔画数为下列汉字归类。Classify the characters according to the number of strokes.

2 strokes：刀、力　　3 strokes：女、子、门　　4 strokes：手、心

5 strokes：田　　6 strokes：米、问、好　　7 strokes：来、男

13 strokes：想

4. 将汉字与对应的意思连起来。Match the characters with their meanings.

米	knife	来	door
刀	rice	力	hand
田	field	手	female
心	to ask	女	to come
子	heart	门	male
好	son	男	to think
问	good	想	strength

5. 给下列汉字标注拼音。Write Pinyin for the following characters.

nǔ	shǒu	dāo	tián	zǐ	nán	lì
女	手	刀	田	子	男	力
xīn	lái	mǐ	hǎo	mén	wèn	xiǎng
心	来	米	好	门	问	想

语音练习

1. 听录音，在听到的音节下划线。Underline the syllables you hear.

cír	cìr	huàr	huār	nàr	nǎr
yèr	yìnr	dǐr	dìr	xīnr	xìnr
gēr	gèr	jiěr	jiér	gǒur	guǒr
gānr	gāngr	huánr	huángr	xiǎoshìr	xiǎojīr

2. 听写拼音。Pinyin dictation.

yìmǐ	wèilái	dāogōng	lìdù	nóngtián	shǒugōng
xīnzàng	nánnǚ	zǐyè	dàmén	hǎohuài	nánxìng
wèntí	xiǎngxiàng	shǒuxù	àihào	cíqì	zuòfàn

3. 听录音补全句子，然后跟读。Listen to the recording, complete the sentences and read them.

1）Xiànzài tīngxiě.

2）Qǐng dǎkāi shū, fān dào dì-yī yè.

3）Qǐng bǎ zuòyè jiāo gěi wǒ.

4）Jīntiān de zuòyè shì shénme?

4. 听录音给下列词或短语标注拼音，并猜猜它们的意思。Listen to the recording, write down the Pinyin for the following words and expressions, and guess their meanings.

xiǎodāo 小刀　xiǎomén 小门　xiǎokǒu 小口　xiǎoshǒu 小 手　bú dà 不大　bú wèn 不 问　bù lái 不来　bù xiǎng 不 想

hǎonán 好 男　hǎonǚ 好 女　hǎoxīnrén 好心人　rì hǎo yuè hǎo 日 好 月 好　shānshuǐ hǎo 山水 好　nǚzǐ hǎo, rìyuè míng 女子 好，日月 明

第六课

练习

1. 给“不”标上实际的声调。Mark the tone of “不” in spoken Chinese.

bù xīn　　bù xiāng　　bù chī　　bù zhī

bù hán　　bù néng　　bù zhí　　bù rú

bù dǒng	bù lǐ	bù zhǐ	bù gěi
bú guì	bú zài	bú xìn	bú lèi

2．听老师的发音，给下列词语标注声调并跟读，注意两组词意义的区别。Listen to the teacher's pronunciation, mark the tones and read after the teacher. Pay attention to the difference between the two groups.

dōngxī	dōngxi
mǎimai	mǎimài
duìtou	duìtóu
dìdào	dìdao

3．听录音，给下列词语标上声调，然后大声朗读，试试在后续的练习中运用这些词汇。Listen to the recording, mark the tones and read aloud. Try to use these words in the following exercises.

Singular	Plural	Possessive case	Honorific form
你 nǐ	你们 nǐmen	你的 nǐde	您 nín
我 wǒ	我们 wǒmen	我的 wǒde	
他 tā	他们 tāmen	他的 tāde	
她 tā	她们 tāmen	她的 tāde	
它 tā	它们 tāmen	它的 tāde	

5．选择填空。Fill in the blanks.

吗　　呢

1）你爸爸、妈妈好__吗__？

2）我爸爸、妈妈很好。你爸爸、妈妈__呢__？

3）他们忙__吗__？

4）我不忙，你__呢__？

6．完成下列对话。Complete the following conversations.

1）A：你忙__吗__？

B：__很忙。/不忙。__

A：你爸爸、妈妈<u>　好吗　</u>？

B：他们<u>　很好　</u>。

2） A：你叫<u>　什么名字　</u>？

B：我叫马丁。你<u>　呢　</u>？

A：我叫小文。你忙吗？

B：<u>很忙。/ 不忙。</u>你呢？

A：<u>我不忙。/ 我很忙。</u>

8. 翻译下列句子。Translation.

1）我很好。

2）我不忙。

3）我叫大明。

4）你叫什么名字？

第七课

练习

1. 给“一”标上实际的声调。Mark the tone of “一” in spoken Chinese.

yì piān	yì shuāng	yìxiē	yì fēn
yì rén	yì qún	yì yuán	yì máo
yì kǒu	yìdiǎn	yìqǐ	yì pǐ
yígòng	yí biàn	yí kuài	yíxià

2. 听录音，在你听到的拼音后打“√”。Listen and mark the one you hear with a “√” after it.

yǎnsè (√)	yánsè ○	zhùzi ○	zhúzi (√)	xiězuò ○	xiézuò (√)
tōngzhī (√)	tóngzhì ○	jiǎnhuà ○	jiǎnghuà (√)	liànxí (√)	liánxì ○
qièshí ○	quèshí (√)	tiān lán ○	tiānrán (√)		

3. 听录音，给下列词语标上声调，然后大声朗读，试试在后续的练习中运用这些词汇。Listen to the recording, mark the tones and read aloud. Try to use these words in the following exercises.

Yīngguó 英国	Fǎguó 法国	Déguó 德国	Xībānyá 西班牙	Hánguó 韩国	Rìběn 日本
Yīngyǔ 英语	Fǎyǔ 法语	Déyǔ 德语	Xībānyáyǔ 西班牙语	Hányǔ 韩语	Rìyǔ 日语

4. 朗读下列句子并标注拼音。Read the following sentences and write down their Pinyin.

1）我介绍一下。 Wǒ jièshào yíxià.
2）他不是学生。 Tā bú shì xuésheng.
3）我也学习汉语。 Wǒ yě xuéxí Hànyǔ.
4）他是我的朋友。 Tā shì wǒ de péngyou.
5）你是英国人吗？ Nǐ shì Yīngguórén ma?

5. 选择填空。Fill in the blanks.

是　×

1）他们学习不__×__忙。
2）我爸爸、妈妈__×__很好。
3）我__是__美国人。
4）她不__是__学生。

是　叫　介绍　的　也　不

1）我__介绍__一下儿，这位__是__林老师。
2）他__叫__大明，是我__的__朋友。
3）我学习汉语，他__也__学习汉语。
4）他__不__是美国人，是英国人。

6. 组词成句。Make sentences with the randomly placed words in each group.

1）忙　也　我们　很　　我们也很忙。
2）吗　也　你　学生　是　　你也是学生吗？
3）也　他们　我的朋友　是　　他们也是我的朋友。
4）不　美国人　我们　是　　我们不是美国人。

7. 完成下列对话。Complete the following conversations.

1）A：老师，请问您贵姓？
B：我姓田，你叫我田老师吧。

2）A：你叫什么名字？
B：我叫马丁。
A：你是哪国人？
B：我是美国人。
A：你是学生吗？
B：我是学生，你也是（学生）吗 / 你呢？
A：我也是学生。

3）A：我介绍一下，这是林老师。
B：林老师，您好！
林老师：你好！你也学汉语吗？
B：对，我也学汉语。

第八课

练习

2. 听录音，说出音节的韵母是左边的还是右边的。Listen to the recording, and tell the finals are on the left or on the right side.

ia	ua
ie	uo
iao	uai
iou	uei

（录音文本：yá、kuā、kuò、yě、zhuā、xiě、jiào、yǒu、guì、guài、shuài、qiāo、jiě、huò、zhuài、zhuī、qiú、huà、jiǔ、jiā、xià、zhuó、yào、shuǐ）

3. 听老师的发音，给下列词语标注声调并跟读。Listen to the teacher's pronunciation, mark the tones and read after the teacher.

bàba	dìdi	jiùjiu	mèimei
māma	gūgu	shūshu	gēge
yéye	jiějie	nǎinai	gōnggong
āyí	wàigōng	wàipó	pópo

4. 听录音，给下列词语标上声调，然后大声朗读，试试在后续的练习中运用这些词汇。Listen to the recording, mark the tones and read aloud. Try to use these words in the following exercises.

Father's side	**Mother's side**
爷爷 yéye	外公 wàigōng
奶奶 nǎinai	外婆 wàipó
叔叔 shūshu	舅舅 jiùjiu
姑姑 gūgu	阿姨 āyí

5. 选择填空。Fill in the blanks.

没　不

1）我<u>没</u>有哥哥，也<u>没</u>有姐姐。

2）他<u>不</u>忙。

3）这<u>不</u>是我们家的照片。

4）我<u>没</u>有女朋友。

5）我的日语<u>不</u>好。

哪　谁　对　有　和　在　现在

1）我的妈妈<u>在</u>美国。

2）<u>谁</u>是你的女朋友？

3）你的女朋友是<u>哪</u>国人？

4）A：你是学生吗？

B：<u>对</u>，我是学生。

5）A：你<u>有</u>女朋友吗？

B：我<u>现在</u>没有女朋友。

6）我的姐姐<u>和</u>妹妹在日本。

6. 根据课文完成下面的对话。Complete the conversations according to the texts.

1）王小文：这是你们<u>家</u>的<u>照片</u>吗？

马丁：对。这是我爸爸，这是我妈妈，这是我<u>妹妹</u>，那是我<u>弟弟</u>。

王小文：她是<u>谁</u>？

马丁：她是我的<u>女朋友</u>。

王小文：她很漂亮！她是<u>哪国</u>人？

马丁：她也是美国人。

2) 王小文：马丁，你<u>有</u>哥哥、姐姐吗？

马丁：我<u>有</u>哥哥，<u>没有</u>姐姐，你呢？

王小文：我没有哥哥，也没有姐姐。

马丁：我爸爸、妈妈、弟弟<u>和</u>妹妹<u>在</u>美国，我哥哥在<u>日本</u>，他学<u>日语</u>。

8. 翻译下列句子。Translation.

1）你有女朋友吗？

2）你有哥哥吗？

3）你的女朋友很漂亮。

4）谁是你的老师？

5）我现在在中国学习汉语。

6）我学习日语和汉语。

第九课

练习

1. 抢答ABC：听老师的发音，指出是A、B、C中的哪一个。做完后再读一读A、B、C三组，注意三者的区别。Interaction: Listen to the teacher's pronunciation, and point out the corresponding Pinyin among A, B, and C. Then read aloud all the columns and pay attention to their differences.

A	B	C	A	B	C
jū	zū	zhū	jì	zì	zhì
qù	cù	chù	qī	cī	chī
xú	sú	shú	xī	sī	shī
juān	zuān	zhuān	jiàn	zàn	zhàn
quàn	cuàn	chuàn	jiāng	zāng	zhāng
xuān	suān	shuān	jiào	zào	zhào
jūn	zūn	zhūn	qiǎo	cǎo	chǎo
qūn	cūn	chūn	xiǎo	sǎo	shǎo

2. 听老师的发音，给下列词语标注声调并跟读。Listen to the teacher's pronunciation, mark the tones and read after the teacher.

lǜshī	jīnglǐ	lǎoshī	xuésheng	yīshēng
kuàijìshī	jiàoshòu	gōngchéngshī	yǎnyuán	shāngrén

3. 听录音，给下列词语标上声调，然后大声朗读，试试在后续的练习中运用这些词汇。Listen to the recording, mark the tones and read aloud. Try to use these words in the following exercises.

hùshi 护士	dàifu 大夫	sījī 司机	jǐngchá 警察	jìzhě 记者	fúwùyuán 服务员

4. 选择填空。Fill in the blanks.

高兴　系　吧　专业　工作　位　个　新　都

1）你做什么＿工作＿？
2）认识你我也很＿高兴＿。
3）这＿个＿学校很好。
4）你们是中国人＿吧＿？
5）我们＿都＿不是中国人。
6）我在中文＿系＿学习汉语。
7）我的＿专业＿是历史。
8）那＿位＿是林老师。

9）他们都是我的 新 朋友。

5. 用“都”改写下面的句子。Paraphrase the following sentences with “都”.

1）我们都是中国人。
2）我们都是老师。
3）我们都不是学生。
4）我们都去美国。
5）他们都学习汉语。

6. 根据课文完成下面的对话。Complete the conversations according to the texts.

1）林老师：我 介绍一下 ，这位是马丁。马丁，这是我的朋友李力。
李力：你好！ 认识你很高兴 ！
马丁：您好！认识您，我也很高兴。 您也是老师吧 ？
李力：不，我是 医生 。这是我的 名片 。你呢？ 你做什么工作 ？
马丁：我是学生，我学习中文。

2）王小文：同学，你的书。
田雨：谢谢！你也是这个学校的学生吧？
王小文：对。我叫王小文。
田雨：我叫田雨。 你学什么专业 ？
王小文：历史。 你们呢 ？
田雨：我的专业是 中国文学 。这是我的同学，我们 都是中文系 的学生。

第十课

练习

2. 听录音，写出拼音并朗读，注意“一”的变调。Listen to the recording, fill in the blanks and read aloud. Pay attention to the sandhi of “一”.

yì zhī bǐ	yì píng shuǐ	yì bǎ dāo	yì běn shū
yí gè zì	yí jiàn shì	yí kuài qián	yí piàn yào

3. 听录音，给下列词语标上声调，然后大声朗读，试试在后续的练习中运用这些词汇。Listen to the recording, mark the tones and read aloud. Try to use these words in the following exercises.

毛	máo	分	fēn	元	yuán	角	jiǎo
零	líng	二	èr	三	sān	六	liù
七	qī	八	bā	九	jiǔ	十	shí
西瓜	xīguā	香蕉	xiāngjiāo	葡萄	pútáo	词典	cídiǎn

4. 听录音，用阿拉伯数字写出钱数。Write down the amounts of money in Arabic numerals according to the recording.

0.20元　　22.00元　　12.20元　　202 元　　112 元

74.40元　　41.70元　　96.60元　　104 元　　200 元

7. 写出下列名词所对应的量词。Write down the measure words for the following nouns.

三个/斤苹果　　两本书　　两个/位医生　　五个面包

三个/位学生　　一个/斤西瓜　　一个人　　两分/角/毛/元/块钱

8. 选择填空。Fill in the blanks.

几　　多少

1）你买 几/多少 个面包？

2）你有 几/多少 本书？

3）你有 几 个弟弟？

4）你们学校有 多少 学生？

9. 根据图示回答问题。Answer the questions according to the pictures.

（1）您买什么？　　我买一本词典。

（2）苹果多少钱一斤？　　苹果两块四（毛钱）一斤。

（3）您还要买什么吗？　　太多了！不要了，谢谢。

（4）一共多少钱？　　一共四十七块五（毛钱）。

10. 完成下列对话。Complete the following conversations.

1）A：请问您买什么？

B：我买面包。多少钱一个？

A：两块五。<u>您买几个</u>？

B：三个。

2）A：<u>您还要什么</u>？

B：不要了，谢谢。<u>一共多少钱</u>？

A：一共十五块钱。

11．翻译下列句子。Translation.

1）请问您买什么？

2）苹果多少钱一斤？/一斤苹果多少钱？/苹果一斤多少钱？

3）您还要什么？

4）一共多少钱？

5）两本书三十块八（毛钱）。

6）给您钱。

总字表*

Character list

B

爸	bà	6
吧	ba	9
白	bái	4
百	bǎi	4
包	bāo	10
北	běi	8
本	běn	4
不	bù	6

C

厂	chǎng	9
词	cí	10

D

大	dà	3
刀	dāo	5
的	de	7
地	dì	6
弟	dì	8
典	diǎn	10
点	diǎn	10
丁	dīng	6
都	dōu	9
对	duì	7
多	duō	9

E

儿	ér	10
二	èr	10

F

法	fǎ	7
饭	fàn	9

G

高	gāo	9
哥	gē	8
个	gè	9
给	gěi	10
工	gōng	9
公	gōng	10
共	gòng	10
贵	guì	7
国	guó	7
果	guǒ	10

H

还	hái	10
孩	hái	8
汉	hàn	6
好	hǎo	5
和	hé	8
很	hěn	6
化	huà	9
火	huǒ	3

J

几	jǐ	10
家	jiā	7
叫	jiào	6

---

* 本表统计如下部分出现的汉字：第3—5课“猜字义，学汉字”板块展示的汉字；第6—10课课文和“字、词、句”板块（除标题、题目要求和注释）出现的所有汉字。
This list includes characters being showed in “guess the meanings and learn characters” part from Lesson 3 to Lesson 5 and all characters in the texts and “character, word, and sentence” part (except for headlines, rubrics and notes) from Lesson 6 to Lesson 10.

姐	jiě	8
介	jiè	7
斤	jīn	10
今	jīn	10
京	jīng	8

K

口	kǒu	3
块	kuài	10

L

来	lái	5
老	lǎo	7
了	le	10
泪	lèi	4
李	lǐ	9
力	lì	5
历	lì	9
两	liǎng	10
亮	liàng	8
林	lín	4
零	líng	10
六	liù	10

M

妈	mā	6
马	mǎ	6
吗	ma	6
买	mǎi	10
忙	máng	6
毛	máo	10
么	me	6
没	méi	8
美	měi	7
妹	mèi	8
门	mén	5
们	men	6
米	mǐ	5
面	miàn	10
名	míng	6
明	míng	4
木	mù	4
目	mù	3

N

哪	nǎ	7
那	nà	8
男	nán	5
呢	ne	6
你	nǐ	6
您	nín	7
女	nǚ	5

P

朋	péng	7
便	pián	10
片	piàn	8
漂	piào	8
苹	píng	10

Q

钱	qián	10
请	qǐng	6

R

人	rén	3
认	rèn	9
日	rì	3

S

三	sān	10
山	shān	3
上	shàng	4
少	shǎo	4
绍	shào	7
谁	shéi	8
什	shén	6
生	shēng	7
师	shī	7

十	shí	10
识	shí	9
史	shǐ	9
是	shì	6
手	shǒu	5
书	shū	8
水	shuǐ	3
四	sì	10

T

他	tā	6
她	tā	6
太	tài	10
天	tiān	3
田	tián	5
同	tóng	7

W

王	wáng	6
位	wèi	9
文	wén	4
问	wèn	5
我	wǒ	6
五	wǔ	10

X

习	xí	7
系	xì	9
下	xià	4
现	xiàn	8
想	xiǎng	5
相	xiàng	4
小	xiǎo	4
校	xiào	9
谢	xiè	9
心	xīn	5
新	xīn	7
兴	xìng	9
姓	xìng	7
学	xué	7

Y

言	yán	7
要	yào	10
也	yě	7
业	yè	9
一	yī	7
医	yī	9
宜	yí	10
意	yì	9
英	yīng	7
友	yǒu	7
有	yǒu	8
雨	yǔ	9
语	yǔ	7
月	yuè	3

Z

在	zài	8
照	zhào	8
这	zhè	7
中	zhōng	7
专	zhuān	9
资	zī	9
子	zǐ	5
字	zì	6
作	zuò	9
做	zuò	9

生词表*

Vocabulary list

B		
爸爸	bàba	6
吧	ba	9/10
本	běn	10
不	bù	6
D		
大家	dàjiā	7
的	de	7
弟弟	dìdi	8
都	dōu	9
对	duì	7
多	duō	9
少	duōshao	10
E		
二十三	èrshísān	10
G		
高兴	gāoxìng	9
哥哥	gēge	8
个	gè	9
给	gěi	10
工作	gōngzuò	9
贵	guì	10
贵姓	guìxìng	7
国	guó	7
H		
还	hái	10
汉语	Hànyǔ	7
和	hé	8
很	hěn	6
J		
几	jǐ	10
家	jiā	8
叫	jiào	6
姐姐	jiějie	8
介绍	jièshào	7
斤	jīn	10
今天	jīntiān	10
K		
块	kuài	10
L		
老师	lǎoshī	7
了	le	10
历史	lìshǐ	9
两	liǎng	10
六	liù	10
M		
妈妈	māma	6
吗	ma	6
买	mǎi	10
忙	máng	6
没	méi	8
没有	méiyǒu	8
美国	Měiguó	7
妹妹	mèimei	8
们	men	6
面包	miànbāo	10
名片	míngpiàn	9

* 本表统计第6—10课课文板块生词框内的生词。
This list includes all the new words in the word boxes from Lesson 6 to Lesson 10.

名字	míngzi	6

N

哪	nǎ	7
那	nà	8
呢	ne	6
你	nǐ	6
你们	nǐmen	8
你好	nǐ hǎo	6
您	nín	7
女朋友	nǚpéngyou	8

P

朋友	péngyou	7
便宜	piányi	10
漂亮	piàoliang	8
苹果	píngguǒ	10

Q

钱	qián	10
请	qǐng	6
请问	qǐngwèn	6

R

认识	rènshi	9
日本	Rìběn	8
日语	Rìyǔ	8

S

谁	shéi	8
什么	shénme	6
十二	shí'èr	10
是	shì	7
书	shū	9
四	sì	10

T

她	tā	6
他们	tāmen	6
太	tài	10
同学	tóngxué	9

W

位	wèi	9
文学	wénxué	9
我	wǒ	6
五	wǔ	10

X

系	xì	9
现在	xiànzài	8
谢谢	xièxie	9
新	xīn	9
姓	xìng	7
学	xué	7
学生	xuésheng	7
学校	xuéxiào	9

Y

要	yào	10
也	yě	7
一	yī	7
一点儿	yīdiǎnr	10
一共	yīgòng	10
一下	yīxià	7
医生	yīshēng	9
英国	Yīngguó	7
有	yǒu	8

Z

在	zài	8
照片	zhàopiàn	8
这	zhè	7
中国	Zhōngguó	9
中文	Zhōngwén	9
专业	zhuānyè	9
做	zuò	9

FLTRP CHINESE LANGUAGE TRAINING SERIES
外研社国际汉语培训教材

Excel in Chinese

“卓越汉语”系列

“卓越汉语”系列教材是外研社针对非学历型外国学生在培训项目中学习基础汉语及专业汉语的实际需求，专门组织国内外多所高等院校及培训机构的教学专家编写，并全新推出的一整套教学资源解决方案。

ISBN 978-7-5135-1474-3

ISBN 978-7-5600-9621-6

“卓越汉语·公司实战篇”专为目前正在或者有意到中国实习或工作的汉语学习者设计，并可供对中国经济问题和商务文化感兴趣的外籍商务人士使用。本教材紧密结合语言学习和商务实际，力求全面提高学习者在商务场合的语言运用能力和跨文化交际能力。同时，穿插介绍中国商务交往的特点、规则以及中国经济背景知识等方面的内容。

“卓越汉语·轻松入门”为综合性基础汉语培训教材，分三册，是以教学媒介语为英语的汉语学习者为对象编写的一套综合性快速入门教材。

“卓越汉语·商务致胜”为综合性商务汉语培训教材，主要供海内外参加培训的外国学生及企业界人士学习商务汉语使用。教材共分五册，各册的教学目标与商务汉语考试（BCT）等级标准相吻合。

ISBN 978-7-5135-1133-9

ISBN 978-7-5135-1416-3

外研汉语网 http://chinese.fltrp.com　　汉加网 http://www.chineseplus.com